Hélène Cixous: Live Theory

Also available in the *Live Theory* series from Continuum:

Hélène Cixous: Live Theory

Ian Blyth

with

Susan Sellers

continuum
NEW YORK • LONDON

CONTINUUM
The Tower Building, 11 York Road, London SE1 7NX
15 East 26th Street, New York, NY 10010

www.continuumbooks.com

British Library Cataloguing-in-Publication Data
A catalogue record for this book is available from the British Library.

ISBN 0-8264-6679-6 (HB)   0-8264-6680-X (PB)

Typeset by Aarontype Limited, Easton, Bristol.
Printed and bound in Great Britain by MPG Books Ltd, Bodmin, Cornwall

Contents

Acknowledgements

Ian Blyth wishes to express his thanks to Susan Sellers for her help in writing this book. Given that Cixous's own writing is created among, with and because of others, it would seem appropriate that this has been a work very much composed 'with' Susan Sellers. I have benefited immeasurably from her encouragement, scholarship, experience and friendship. Throughout the long process of writing, reading and rewriting, she has gone through each draft of the book with meticulous attention – offering numerous suggestions, anecdotes, comments and snippets of text. This book could not have been written without her. Any faults that remain are entirely my own. Among the many others who have been there along the way, I would especially like to thank my parents, for their continued support over the years, as well as Gill Plain and Anna Paterson, for their helpful insights and observations.

We would both like to take this opportunity to once again thank Hélène Cixous for her participation in the interview and for all the other ways, consciously or unconsciously, she has contributed to this book. We are also grateful for the efforts of Tristan Palmer (a dynamic and understanding editor) and Christina Parkinson, both of Continuum Books. As it always does, the School of English at the University of St Andrews provided valuable material assistance. Beverley Bie Brahic very kindly allowed us to read (and quote from) the manuscript of her forthcoming translation of *Le jour où je n'étais pas là*.

Finally, Susan Sellers would like to offer her thanks to the Leverhulme Trust for the award of a Research Fellowship. Her involvement in this project is one outcome of their generous support.

Chapter 1

Introduction

In January 1998 Hélène Cixous writes a letter to Martin McQuillan, one of the editors of a collection of essays on the subject of 'Post-Theory'.[1] She is writing in response to his request for an epilogue to the volume, but Cixous feels unable to write the piece – the topic is too immense; to do it justice, she says, would require 'a book-length book' (p. 210). Instead, Cixous offers some hints on what she might have written (and explains why she has not done so). She takes as her starting point the world of difference between the Anglo-American concept of '*Theory*' and its French counterpart, '*Théorie*' (p. 210). On the one hand, because she is 'a writer', 'a *poet*', Cixous finds herself relating '(*negatively*) to *théorie* in France' (p. 210). On the other hand, she feels that she must 'side with all of you [in England and the USA] who have to defend what is construed under that name against the Philistines' (p. 210). The word '*Theory*', Cixous considers, has 'had ambiguous fortunes during the twentieth century in English speaking countries' (p. 210). For the last four decades, she adds, 'this term has belonged to the lexicon of the intra-academic ideological war' (p. 211). It has been the subject of unfavourable connotations in some fields, welcomed as a positive advancement in others and has been met with complete indifference elsewhere. Cixous goes on to describe an incident from her early childhood: the experience of watching a column of ants progressing along the ground with 'burdens on their backs' (p. 212). Cixous drifts in and out of the column: she is 'an isolated ant', 'a line of porters is formed in the paths of her dream', the line is in a state of ambivalence, 'discontinuous continuous', 'words move, take turns, go around each other, climb' (p. 212). Cixous calls this dream-vision-memory 'her first theory' (p. 212). It is, perhaps un-wittingly (but probably quite deliberately), typical of the elusive, enigmatic, and (to some eyes) strange practice of Cixous's theor-etical writing. Cixous's final (unwritten) section 'would have been a prosopopoeia of Theoria' (p. 212). Prosopopoeia is another word for personification (of an abstract thing); it can also be a speech introducing or taking the place of an imaginary, absent or dead person. Cixous plays with both aspects of the word (theory is per-sonified as 'Theoria', but it is also absent, missing – Cixous admits that she hasn't written this section). In 'Post-Word', Cixous draws the reader into the text, unweaving, substituting and extrapolat-ing. She then leaves the reader, freeing them, forcing them to find their own way out (their own interpretation). As an approach to theory it is far from conventional. But then Cixous has created a very different kind of theory. And Hélène Cixous is something very different from the usual kind of theoretician.

The 'Anglo-American' Cixous

Different linguistic communities frequently have different percep-tions of a writer's work. Hélène Cixous is no exception to this rule. In the English-speaking world her name is more often than not associated with two texts, both published in 1975 (but translated a decade apart): 'Le Rire de la Méduse' and 'Sorties'. 'Le Rire de la Méduse' first appears in a special 'Simone de Beauvoir' edition of the journal *L'Arc*.[2] A revised version of 'Le Rire de la Méduse' is translated in 1976 as 'The Laugh of the Medusa' and published in one of the first volumes of the American feminist journal *Signs*.[3] Its inclusion four years later in Elaine Marks and Isabelle de Cour-trivon's anthology *New French Feminisms* (1980) brings 'Medusa' to an even wider audience.[4] As does its publication in *The Signs Reader* in 1983.[5] 'Sorties' first appears in Cixous and Catherine Clément's *La Jeune Née*: a collaborative project and one in a series of texts pub-lished under the rubric of 'Féminin futur'.[6] *La Jeune Née* is divided into three sections: Clément's 'La Coupable' (pp. 7–13); Cixous's 'Sorties' (pp. 114–246); and 'Échange' – a lively dialogue between the two women (pp. 247–96). The dialogic nature of the volume is worth remembering as numerous critics make the synecdochical leap from 'Sorties' to *La Jeune Née* – thereby erasing Catherine Clément's contribution. A brief excerpt from 'Sorties' was published in translation in 1977;[7] another short passage appeared three years later in Marks and de Courtrivon's *New French Feminisms*.[8] The whole essay finally appears in English, as 'Sorties: Out and Out: Attacks/Ways Out/Forays', in Betsy Wing's 1986 translation of *The Newly Born Woman*.[9]

Although there are also many substantial differences between the two texts, 'Medusa' and 'Sorties' share a common purpose and a good deal of common material (a not unknown nor unusual circumstance in Cixous's writing, where her texts lead into and out of each other creating a complex web of allusion and meaning). Both essays are at least partly concerned with the means and methods by which patriarchal society posits women as 'other' – how patriarchy consistently denies women the right to individual existence and expression (see Chapter 2). What Cixous does in response is to envision a new form of writing – *écriture féminine* (feminine writing) – that is outside of and no longer bound by the rules of patriarchal discourse. Cixous borrows freely from the discourses of satire and polemic, humour and philosophy, psychoanalysis and sexuality – weaving these discourses in and out of her own discoveries, using whatever she feels that she needs to put her ideas across. 'Medusa' and 'Sorties' are significant texts in this process. They offer important insights into Cixous's thoughts on how an *écriture féminine* might be achieved. Yet, they are not the be-all and end-all of the story. Nevertheless, in the years following their translation these two essays have all too frequently – and mistakenly – been put forward as somehow representative of Cixous's entire oeuvre. In numerous critical works, the Cixous presented to readers is reduced to a sketchy caricature – one or two pages, paragraphs, sentences or phrases from one or other of these essays. The same quotations predictably recur, again and again, doing much to limit the perception and reception of the rest of Cixous's work and ideas. It is still regrettably true to say that for a significant section of the Anglo-American community, if Cixous is known at all, she is known only as the author of 'Medusa' and/or 'Sorties'.

Cixous's exasperation with the limitations of her Anglo-American reputation comes across loudly in an interview, first published in 1994, with the French-Canadian scholar Mireille Calle-Gruber.[10] Speaking about the expectations that these texts have created and the frequency with which she is still asked about them, Cixous says:

> I was inspired to write those essays by the urgency of a moment in the general discourse concerning 'sexual difference' . . . I would never have thought, when I began writing, that one day I would find myself making strategic and even military gestures: constructing a camp with lines of defence! It's a gesture which is foreign to me.   (p. 5)

Cixous does not express regret at having written these texts. As she explains: 'To "defend" is sometimes a necessity' (p. 6). Yet, she feels that the incessant reference to them, and to the texts that are most similar to them, at the expense of the rest of her oeuvre, 'produces errors of evaluation, because to have an upright position, analogous to that of a theoretician, is not my intention' (p. 7). Cixous remarks to Calle-Gruber that she 'left [her] own ground' in writing 'Medusa' and 'Sorties' (p. 5). This does not mean that they witnessed a change in her political commitment, merely that when she came to write these essays Cixous changed the manner in which her political commitment was expressed. Whereas Cixous's early theory sets up so-called lines of defence, her present 'field of action' or 'combat', Mireille Calle-Gruber concludes, is situated in her 'poetic writing, language, fiction' (p. 7). These 'poetic' texts require a certain amount of work on the part of the reader that is not always the case in Cixous's more overtly theoretical work, but the effort of reading these more problematic texts is well rewarded. It is one of the paradoxes of Cixous's oeuvre that the texts which reveal the most about the nature of *écriture féminine* are often those that appear, at first glance, the least theoretically minded. It is with this in mind that a substantial amount of this current book on Cixous's 'theory' will be taken up with a discussion of Cixous's fiction and theatrical writing (see Chapter 3).

The 'real' Hélène Cixous

Hélène Cixous is a writer of great variety. A creator of works of fiction,[11] a playwright, a theoretician, a librettist, screenwriter, critic, reviewer, philosopher, poet, political activist, humanitarian, academic, cultural commentator, autobiographical chronicler – her work is spread across many fields of writing and being. The notion that one segment of her writing can have priority, can be separated from all of the rest, does not, on close examination, hold much water. Each aspect of Cixous's writing is in dialogue with and dependent upon all of the many other aspects that come together to make up her oeuvre. Through this constellation, this coming together of texts, a certain interconnectedness is formed – an inter-connectedness that extends to texts by other writers with whom Cixous has developed an almost symbiotic, very loving relation-ship over the years (see esp. Chapter 5). The voices of Cixous's texts possess a life independent of their author. Quotations, paraphrases, allusions, parodies and acts of textual ventriloquism lie side by side with what might be conventionally called authorial comments. Her texts are multi-vocal and kaleidoscopic. Who it is that is speaking at any particular point is not always abundantly clear. This situation is further complicated when one realizes that the normal rules of genre have broken down. Running one's eyes over this or that text, it cannot always be said whether one is reading a work of fiction or theatre or theory. Everything is woven into the same fabric of writing. Uneasy with the idea of limits, ignoring conventions, boundaries and rules, difficult but rewarding, serious, playful, humorous, poetic, even, on occasion, self-contradictory, Cixous's writing has a complex and luminous quality that is always just eluding definition. Much of this derives from her different approach to the questions of subject matter, character, form, style and so on. It is fair to say that there is plenty of scope for such differ-ence – her output is frankly prodigious. In French alone (the lan-guage in which the vast majority of her texts have been written), she has over 60 book-length publications, plus more than 150 articles to her name. Cixous has also been translated into many other languages, including Brazilian, Danish, Dutch, German, Italian,

Japanese, Norwegian, Polish, Slovak, Spanish, Swedish and, of course, English.[12]

The language of *écriture féminine*

The roots of language go deep, supplying the essential nutrients of writing. As Cixous tells Mireille Calle-Gruber, she believes no-one 'can write without having benefited from a childhood gift of language' (*Rootprints*, p. 38). Cixous was born in 1937 in the town of Oran. A port on the Mediterranean coast, Oran lies in the north west of what was the then French colony of Algeria (following a long, extremely bitter and destructive war, Algeria became an independent nation in 1962 – see below). Cixous's family background is mixed. Both her mother, Eve Cixous (*née* Klein), and her maternal grandmother, known to the family as Omi, were of Ashkenazy, Eastern European descent. Her father, Georges Cixous, came from a Mediterranean Sephardic Jewish background (his grandparents having moved to Oran from Morocco in the nineteenth century). Her mother and grandmother both spoke German: the lingua franca of Eastern European Jews. Her father's first language was French, but he also spoke Spanish. Since her grandmother did not speak French very well, at home the family would converse in German. In 'Albums and Legends', a memoir of her childhood years, Cixous recalls that her Francophone father adapted well to this circumstance and 'forged, in a Joycian way, an entire system on the German language that became part of the family idiom'.[13] Cixous believes that her own respect for and love of language, her own 'verbal virtuosity or versatility', can be traced back to these days (*Rootprints*, p. 198). As she recalls in another memoir of her childhood years, 'My Algeriance, in other words: to depart not to arrive from Algeria', her mother and father 'passed with pleasure and deftness from one language to the other' – conversing in French, German, Spanish, English, Arabic and Hebrew.[14] Consequently, although Cixous writes in French, she does so, by her own admission, as an outsider. Cixous's doctorate and professorial chair are in English Literature. She reads Brazilian and Russian fluently and has a working knowledge of numerous other languages, including Greek and Latin. Therefore, because of her German mother and grandmother, her linguistically playful father, and her own polyglottism, she has what she calls 'a foreign relationship to the French language' (*Rootprints*, p. 84). It is from this foreignness, she considers, that writing emerges. Cixous admits that she feels most at home in the sounds and rhythms of German, her 'mother tongue', but her writing needs that slight *frisson* of distance and strangeness that can only be found, for her, in French.

This intimate connection between her writing and the French language creates a number of difficulties for the reader of Cixous in translation. When writing moves across languages, changes occur. Words and phrases that are essential to one language, have no equivalent in another. This is all the more significant in the case of a writer such as Cixous, for language is not just the medium in which she creates her texts: it is the site of a political struggle. Cixous's writing is packed with neologisms, portmanteau words, puns, alliterations and poetic repetitions; she also plays with grammatical genders, often reversing them (nouns in French can be either 'masculine' or 'feminine' – a distinction that does not exist in English). Cixous is a great believer in the power and potentiality of language. As she admits to Mireille Calle-Gruber, language is 'terrifying' and 'intoxicating' in its economy: 'displace a letter, a full stop, a comma, and everything changes. Out to infinity' (*Rootprints*, p. 22). Cixous's comment brings to light a significant problem. If language is balanced on such a knife's edge of possibility that individual signs can harbour immeasurable power, what kind of effect is created when one moves an entire text from one language into another? One possible danger might be that all sense is lost – or at least distorted beyond all reasonable recognition. This is, up to a point, exactly what happens. As Cixous explains in an interview conducted in 1999, the fact that she is one of those 'writers who are adventurous in language' means that her texts, to a certain extent, are all but 'untranslatable'.[15] A translator cannot hope to accurately reproduce one of Cixous's texts in another language. At least, not word for word. Instead, Cixous explains:

> It requires a person who knows about the issues and who has an ear for languages. And, since you cannot save or preserve the special effects in language (I mean the signifiers), you cannot find

> equivalence in the arrival language, you have to look for
> equivalence by displacing the effects.   (p. 339)

Translators of Cixous must therefore be prepared to improvise. They must, in Cixous's words, 'be faithful by being unfaithful' (p. 339). Translation occurs through dialogue and interaction. This process, when it is operating at its best, involves both languages, both parties, translator and author, in the creation of the finished piece. However, while it is often possible for Cixous to 'discuss things in sympathy with a translator', allowing both author and translator to search for 'equivalence', this is not always the case (p. 339). It is thus, Cixous says, on occasion necessary for the 'translator to take the risk and the responsibility, to give up something here and, on the contrary, invent something there' (p. 339).

This process of revision and invention can be seen operating in Cixous's 1979 text, *Vivre l'orange/To Live the Orange*, which is published in a bilingual edition (the English text is given on the even numbered left-hand pages, the French text on the odd numbered right-hand ones).[16] *Vivre l'orange* is noteworthy not only because it encourages comparisons by printing a parallel text, but also because Cixous reworks Ann Liddle and Sarah Cornell's translation – creating a situation where the two texts flow into and out of each other with various degrees of shading. This produces a variety of interesting effects. Languages intermix. 'Appeler ⟨⟨tu⟩⟩ chaque chose' in the 'French' text (p. 103) becomes 'To call each thing ⟨⟨tu⟩⟩, *o du! voce! tu! εσν*' in the 'English' (p. 102). Over the page, the word '*voce!*' in the 'French' text (p. 105) becomes '*o du!*' in the 'English' (p. 104); '*voce!*' then appears later on in the 'English' text (p. 104) at a point where there is no equivalent word in the 'French'. With these and many other inflections and alterations one can see that in *Vivre l'orange* Cixous is painting in language with very loose and lively brushstrokes. At numerous points she plays with the sense and sound of words. The words 'Orange' and 'Oran' (Cixous's birthplace), 'Pomme' and 'Apple', move freely from one text into the other – giving up something here, inventing something else there (see, for example, pp. 64–5). Perhaps most significantly, at one point the phrase 'I am foreigne' appears out of nowhere in the English text (p. 40) – again, without an equivalent phrase in the French text. This inclusion of foreignness within the 'foreign' (i.e. non-French) text can be seen as Cixous creating her own version of one of her father's Joycean jokes. The word 'foreigne' looks as if it has been invented by Joyce. His works would have been extremely familiar to Cixous. The main strand of her doctoral research was on Joyce and her vast doctorat d'Etat, published in 1969 as *L'Exil de James Joyce ou l'art du remplacement* (*The Exile of James Joyce or the Art of Replacement*), had been twice the length of a standard French doctoral thesis.[17] However, 'foreigne' is also a politicized play on grammatical gender. In French, the adjective 'foreign' can be either masculine (*étranger*) or feminine (*étrangère*). By adding an '-e' to the end of the English word 'foreign', Cixous creates the equivalent of a 'feminine' adjective in English.[18] In highlighting the femininity of the foreign, Cixous is perhaps alluding to her own 'foreign relationship' with French – suggesting that this idea of the foreign emerges not only from her family background, but also from the fact that she is a woman. As a woman, she is a stranger, an other, a person who is outside of the masculine signifying economy (see Chapter 2). 'I am foreigne' in the English text evokes the idea that 'as a woman, I do not "belong" in the French language' – hence the need for an/other 'language', *écriture féminine*.

As the above suggests, no amount of notation, no matter how thorough it may be, can hope to convey all of the themes and variations in one of Cixous's texts. A balance has to be maintained between the desire to explain what is going on and the necessity to leave space for the text itself to be heard (or not heard – at least not on a 'conscious' level). It follows that when Cixous's writing is translated or transferred out of its original language(s) something will be lost. The many poetic nuances of her work are especially difficult to get across. However, as Cixous has become more well known and appreciated in other, non-French linguistic communities, so have the opportunities for more subtle and 'unfaithfully faithful' translations of her work increased. This is particularly the case in English, where Cixous is more often than not, at some level or another, involved in the translation process. Therefore, as this current book primarily addresses an English-speaking audience, it will draw most of its examples and points of discussion from the better, more extensive English translations of Cixous that now exist. Where it has been necessary to quote from a text only avail-able in French, a translation of the passage is provided in square brackets immediately following the original text.

Algeria

Hélène Cixous has written a number of times, movingly, about her childhood encounters with anti-Semitism.[19] In a text entitled 'Coming to Writing', she writes: 'I had the "luck" to take my first steps in the blazing hotbed between two holocausts, in the midst, in the very bosom of racism, to be three years old in 1940, to be Jewish, one part of me in the concentration camps, one part of me in the "colonies"'.[20] The spread of European fascism – particu-larly the growing power of Hitler in Germany (which led to the Second World War and the Holocaust) – overshadowed her first few years. The emergence of Algerian nationalism blighted the later years of her childhood. During the war, because he was a Jew, Cixous's father, a doctor, was prevented from practising his profession by the Vichy régime. Barred from school, Cixous was educated at home (even after the war, for a long time she was the only Jewish pupil in her class at the Lycée).[21] Many members of her extended family perished in concentration camps at the hands of the Nazis (see *Rootprints*, pp. 190–5). Following the war, Cixous's father, in what she calls 'a gesture of great freedom', moved the family from Oran to Algiers (*Stigmata*, p. 160). Choosing not to live in any of the 'French' parts of the city, they settled in the 'Algerian' district of the Clos Salembier. While her father was alive, an uneasy peace was established with their 'Arab' neighbours. After Cixous's father died in 1948 from tuberculosis (he was only 39 years of age), something resembling a state of 'daily siege' ensued (p. 189). The corpses of cats and dogs were thrown over the wall surrounding their garden. Cixous and her brother Pierre were chased, beaten and, once, spat upon in the street. As Cixous remarks in 'My Alger-iance', isolation, enclosure, alienation and intolerance became the dominant themes: 'never were we "inhabitants" of this neigh-borhood ... the 50,000 indigenous people fifty meters from us remained impenetrable' (p. 160).

The experiences that surrounded the early death of Cixous's father leave a strong imprint on both her life and work. It is often remarked that Cixous's first work of fiction, *Dedans* (translated as *Inside*), winner of the Prix Médicis in 1969, is the first of what will be many attempts to come to terms with and write about the death and lasting memory of her father.[22] In an article entitled 'From the Scene of the Unconscious to the Scene of History' (the translation of a lecture given at the University of Utrecht in June 1987), Cixous herself comments that *Inside* 'was necessarily written within the father, in seeking him right up to death and *revenant* (coming back, ghostly)'.[23] In writing *Inside*, Cixous seeks out the origins of the 'I' – running back along the path of the psychological traces that have led to the person who lives in the present. Unsurprisingly, Cixous's description of this quest in 'From the Scene of the Unconscious . . .' is expressed in distinctly psychoanalytical terms: ' "I" am in the father I carry within me, he haunts me, I live him. There is a rapport between the father and language, the father and the "symbolic" ' (p. 4). Yet, while *Inside* charts the emergence of the subject, the effect of the experiences of loss and death, and the journey out of the primal or pre-Oedipal scene into the 'Symbolic' of language (see Chapter 2), it also investigates the effects of an intolerant and repressive society. The process of discovery and self-realization takes place firstly through a meditation, as a child, about the death of the father; and then, in the second section of *Inside*, with the 'I', now an adult, returning to the city of her childhood. As with so many of Cixous's texts, the line between life and fiction is stretched so thin as to be almost non-existent. Following a brief epigrammatic passage, the first section of the text opens with the words: 'MY HOUSE IS SURROUNDED. IT IS ENCIRCLED BY THE IRON GRATING. INSIDE, we live. Outside, they are fifty thousand, they surround us' (p. 7). The image is both metaphorical (in that it can be said to represent the womb-like state of the pre-Oedipal mother/child dyad) and also autobiographical – it reaches back to her memories of life in the Clos Salembier.

Following the death of her husband, Cixous's mother trained and then practised as a midwife. Cixous frequently accompanied her mother in her work and witnessed many women giving birth.

In 'Coming to Writing' Cixous remarks that she has 'always taken pleasure in watching a woman give birth' (p. 30). In 1955 Cixous married and, in the years between 1958 and 1961, had three children of her own – one daughter and two sons (one of her sons died after a year of troubled life). In both witnessing and experiencing childbirth, Cixous was struck with the manner in which maternity allows women the unique experience of sharing a body with another person. This capacity she saw in women, this special relationship to the 'other' that can be experienced through motherhood, proved to be an extremely important consideration when Cixous came to map out her theoretical terrain (see Chapter 2). In 'Coming to Writing' Cixous compares the psychic processes and effects of writing and childbirth (the original French title of the essay, 'La Venue à l'écriture', can also be translated as 'Her Arrival/Birth in Writing').[24] Arguing that writing is formed out of 'flesh that lets strangeness come through' (*Coming to Writing*, pp. 38–9), Cixous comments that her motivation in bringing this writing into being 'is analogous to what moves the mother to write the universe so that the child will grasp and name it' (p. 51).

Cixous is ambivalent in her attitude to Algeria. This ambivalence even extends to her name, Cixous – 'unpronounceable' in French, it turns out to be 'the name of a Berber tribe' (*Stigmata*, p. 158). In 'From the Scene of the Unconscious . . .' Cixous writes that the 'foreignness, exile, war, the phantom memory of peace, mourning and pain' she experienced as a child in Algeria taught her 'that human roots know no borders' (p. 2). Following her marriage in 1955 (she divorced in 1964), Cixous left Algiers and moved to Paris, where she began to work towards the *agrégation* in English (a prestigious examination for teachers). Her move to France is significant in many ways. In the first place, as she remarks in 'Albums and Legends', 'the anti-Semitism was incomparably weaker in Paris than in Algiers' (p. 204). However, as soon as she emerged from beneath its shadow, another exclusion rose up to take its place: 'I abruptly learned that my unacceptable truth in this world was my being a woman. Right away, it was war. I felt the explosion, the odour of misogyny' (p. 204). From this point onwards, she remarks, she 'adopted an imaginary nationality which is a literary nationality' (p. 204). Cixous became 'a writer', 'a poet'. Her brother, a medical student, left Algeria in 1961 in order to complete his studies in Bordeaux (he returned, briefly, in 1962). Cixous's mother, on the other hand, stayed on in Algeria throughout the war and in the years after independence. During the war many French houses in Algeria were burned down by the nationalist Front de libération nationale (FLN). It is rumoured that Cixous's mother's house only escaped this fate because she was the local midwife (see *Stigmata*, p. 160). Nevertheless, her mother was eventually expelled from the country in 1971, along with the other remaining 'French' Algerians.

France

In 1959 Cixous passed her *agrégation*. She taught *lycée* (secondary school) for several years, before taking up junior posts at the University of Bordeaux and then the Sorbonne in Paris. In 1960 she began to write a doctoral thesis on James Joyce, supervised by Jean-Jacques Mayoux. Two years later, in 1962, Cixous met Jacques Derrida. He was also just embarking on a career as a writer and it was the start of a long association between the two of them (see Chapters 4 and 5). As Cixous tells Mireille Calle-Gruber, she and Derrida 'are often attracted, interested, questioned, moved or disturbed by the same mysteries' (*Rootprints*, p. 81). In 1967, despite the fact that she had not yet completed her doctorate (she did so the next year), Cixous was appointed to a professorship in English Literature at the University of Nanterre. Soon afterwards, following the events of May 1968, Cixous was closely involved in the process of setting up the experimental University of Paris VIII in the district of Vincennes (since 1978 Paris VIII has been located in Saint-Denis). Taking full advantage of the relatively free hand given to her, she oversaw the appointment to the faculty of, among others, Gilles Deleuze, Gérard Genette, Michel Foucault, Tzvetan Todorov and a number of Latin-American writers. Cixous was also involved, with Genette and Todorov, in setting up the journal *Poétique*. The next year she was herself appointed to a professorship in English Literature at Paris VIII and in 1974 started up a doctoral programme in *Etudes Féminines*. It was the first such programme in Europe and it has endured a troubled history. Granted 'official' status at times, the programme has had its accreditation removed at others – all depending upon the ideological stance of the government in power at any given moment. Its official status is still uncertain (in June 2002 the current Chirac administration once again refused to recognize the doctoral programme in *Etudes Féminines*). In response to these upheavals, in 1980 Cixous created the Centre de Recherches en Etudes Féminines. The Centre offers a number of undergraduate and postgraduate programmes. In addition to these programmes, Cixous takes a doctoral research seminar (although this is intended to lead to a doctorate within the Centre, the seminar is also a space in which to engage in high level research without necessarily working towards a formal qualification – many of the people who attend the seminar already have doctorates from other institutions). Exploring a different theme or topic each year, reading texts by both men and women, these seminars are attended by scholars and postgraduates from all over the world. Three collections of translations from Cixous's seminars are available in English (see Chapter 5).[25]

After meeting Antoinette Fouque, one of the founders of the Mouvement de Libération des Femmes (MLF), in 1975 Cixous took the political choice to publish her work exclusively with Fouque's publishing house Des femmes. Aside from a number of theatrical works, one collection of essays and several works of fiction, this exclusive association with Des femmes continued for over two decades (Cixous's current publisher is Galilée). Another important literary encounter took place in 1977, when Cixous was shown examples of the work of the Brazilian writer Clarice Lispector (see Chapters 3 and 5; unfortunately, Cixous and Lispector never met in person – Lispector died from cancer at the end of 1977). Cixous was overwhelmed and overjoyed by what she read: she found in Lispector, for the first time, a woman who approached writing in the very manner she had been describing in her own theoretical work (up to this point, all of Cixous's major examples had come from male writers – Shakespeare, Kleist, Kafka, Genet, etc.). In the early 1980s Ariane Mnouchkine asked Cixous to write for the Théâtre du Soleil. Cixous's collaboration with Mnouchkine and the Théâtre du Soleil helped to bring fresh impetus and direction to her theoretical writing (see Chapter 3). Throughout the

1990s, while continuing to teach at Paris VIII, Cixous undertook a number of visiting professorships in North America. She was given honorary doctorates from universities in the United States, Canada, England and Scotland; she was also awarded the *Légion d'Honneur* in 1994. Since the early 1990s an increasing number of Cixous's texts have made the transition into English. Her work is recognized for its rich interdisciplinary appeal: connecting with such fields as literature, philosophy, divinity, social anthropology and gender studies. Hélène Cixous continues to write, dividing her time between Paris and the South of France.

This book will not offer an overall survey of Cixous's oeuvre (an impossible task for a short volume of this kind). Instead, with reference to certain key texts, it will concern itself with Cixous's theoretical approach to writing – *écriture féminine* – as it develops and changes over the years. The next chapter, 'Feminine writing', will look in detail at Cixous's essay 'Sorties' (and several other texts) in order to trace the outline of the theory of *écriture féminine* as it was in the mid-1970s. It will show that at the heart of *écriture féminine* lies the desire to set up a non-acquisitional space – a space where the self can explore and experience the non-self (the 'other') in mutual respect, harmony and love. A 'feminine' approach to the other is generous and giving, it avoids the ('masculine') impulse to appropriate or annihilate the other's difference, allowing the other to remain as 'other'. While arguing that it is easier for women to adopt such a 'feminine' approach to writing, Cixous does not see *écriture féminine* as the sole domain of women. Wary of the connotations of 'masculine' and 'feminine', Cixous re-situates her theory within non-gender-specific 'libidinal economies'. Cixous is keen to emphasize that *écriture féminine* is a 'practice' of writing. The chapter on Cixous's fiction and theatre (Chapter 3) will look at a selection of Cixous's fiction and theatrical texts in order to explore how the ideas that come to make up *écriture féminine* connect with and change within these genres over the years. Starting with the early texts, it will look at the seeming disparity between Cixous's 'theory' and practice in these texts. It will argue that the early texts are engaged in a necessary project of self-exploration and experimentation – paving the way for an *écriture féminine*. The texts of the late

1970s, early 1980s will be considered, before turning to look at Cixous's work with the Théâtre du Soleil in the mid-1980s (whose importance has already been mentioned). The discussion will then round off with an exploration of Cixous's writing from the late 1980s onwards – showing that although her more recent work appears to have achieved the ideal of a 'writing of the other', new concerns and issues have entered into the space of her writing. Chapter 4, 'Poetic theory', will look in detail at one of these concerns: the growing sense of urgency which is attached to the idea of the 'poetic' in Cixous's work. It will expand upon what Cixous means by 'a poet' and the 'poetic'. With reference to her more recent essays on poetic writing, this chapter will consider how the idea of an *écriture féminine* has progressed and altered since its appearance on the scene in the mid-1970s. Cixous's recent essays show an increased interest in the economy of the 'unknown', in the act of writing as-it-is-happening, in the impossibility of 'capturing' and preserving the passing instant, and in the role of dreams in the creation of her texts. The similarities and differences between Cixous's poetic approach to writing and the philosophical twistings and turnings of Jacques Derrida's writing will also be discussed. Chapter 5, 'Cixous on others: others on Cixous' will look at Cixous's literary criticism, particularly her work with the seminars at the Centre de Recherches en Etudes Féminines. Taking Cixous's reading of/with Clarice Lispector as a starting point, it will show how Cixous's belief in the interconnections between reading and writing that are revealed in her critical work has important implications for the rest of her oeuvre. This chapter will also include a discussion of the range of critical writing about Cixous that is currently available (a number of critical monographs on Cixous are available in English; among the many shorter pieces on her writing there have been important and insightful contributions by Mireille Calle-Gruber and Jacques Derrida). These chapters 'on' Cixous will be followed by a chapter 'with' Cixous – a previously unpublished interview with Hélène Cixous conducted in Paris in June 2002 (Chapter 6, 'Cixous live'). In this interview Cixous discusses her influences and inspirations, her thoughts on the nature of writing and her belief in the need for an ethical relationship with the world. The interview also illuminates and expands upon many of the points that are discussed in the rest of the book. The book concludes with a comprehensive bibliography, giving Cixous's French book-length publications and the many translations of her work available in English (book-length publications, articles and interviews). The bibliography also lists a selection of the many books and articles that have been written on or about Hélène Cixous.

Chapter 2

Feminine writing

I will say: today writing is woman's.
> (*The Newly Born Woman*, p. 85)

The variety of creative, poetic, philosophical and theoretical approaches that are collected under the rubric of *écriture féminine* run in a semi-continuous thread throughout Cixous's oeuvre. To explain what links such a constellation of ideas is far from easy. In particular, it is far from simple to say what, exactly, it is that *écriture féminine* 'is' or 'does'. As Cixous comments in her 1975 essay, 'Sorties': 'At the present time, *defining* a feminine practice of writing is impossible with an impossibility that will continue; for this practice will never be able to be *theorized*, enclosed, coded, which does not mean it does not exist' (p. 92). This sentence has been widely quoted – and rightly so, for it gets to the very heart of the matter with deceptive simplicity. There are a host of ways in which Cixous's caveat can be and has been read, but perhaps the most significant word to focus on is 'practice'. One cannot say exactly what *écriture féminine* is, so the argument goes; one can merely observe *écriture féminine* in the act of doing what it does – it is, quite literally, an 'experimental' approach to writing (as will become apparent later on, the word experimental is operating on several levels of meaning here). Given that Cixous then adds that this 'practice' of *écriture féminine* 'takes place and will take place somewhere other than in the territories subordinated to philosophical-theoretical domination' (p. 92), the question arises: is it right and proper to refer to *écriture féminine* as 'theory' at all?

The short answer is yes, but with reservations. That is to say, *écriture féminine* is not a theory as such (at least not in the sense in which theory is commonly understood), but something that is still related to theory. By placing it outside of the 'territories' of theory, Cixous sets up a relativistic relationship with these very territories. In other words, *écriture féminine*'s difference from theory requires that it has certain things in common with theory. There need to be points of similarity, or relata, in order for contrasts between one thing and another to be made – if there are no such relata, then any comparison is empty and meaningless. Therefore, *écriture féminine* is, to a certain extent, 'theoretical'. However, Cixous encourages the non-theoretical, empirical aspects of *écriture féminine* to come to the fore in order to make a point. She wishes to assert a claim to a degree of independence, to highlight the difference of *écriture féminine* from other, more traditional forms of theory. Consequently, although she does not offer a (potentially restrictive) formula-to-be-followed, Cixous does give various hints and suggestions about the nature of *écriture féminine*. Initially difficult to unpack and decipher, these hints and suggestions prove to be very illuminating – much more illuminating in fact than a common or garden definition would ever have been. The irony is, while claiming that *écriture féminine* is 'impossible' to theorize, Cixous's descriptions of *écriture féminine* in 'Sorties' actually do a very good job of introducing the basics of her 'theory'. At least, that is, in its early days. As will be discussed in later chapters, Cixous constantly refines and alters her ideas about *écriture féminine* over the course of the years (see Chapters 3 and 4).

The feminine Imaginary

After explaining in 'Sorties' that *écriture féminine* will 'never be able to be *theorized*, enclosed, coded', Cixous remarks that in lieu of such an explanation, 'one can begin to speak. Begin to point out some effects, some elements of unconscious drives, some relations of the feminine Imaginary to the Real, to writing' (p. 92). Several of the words Cixous uses here require some clarification. While on the whole eschewing the often bewildering jargon that was a feature of much of the academic and theoretical writing of the 1970s (a tendency which arguably did more harm than good when it came to the wider dissemination of the ideas and insights contained in this writing), Cixous was, and still is, extremely interested in the radical creative and interpretative possibilities that emerge from within psychoanalytical theories.

The 'Imaginary' and the 'Real', for instance, are two of the three overlapping stages in the French post-Freudian psychoanalyst Jacques Lacan's theory of childhood development – the third stage is known as the 'Symbolic'.[1] The Imaginary can be thought of as the non- or pre-verbal state of existence the child inhabits before the 'resolution' of the Oedipus complex. In the Imaginary, the child has developed the beginnings of a sense of individual self – what Lacan calls the *moi*, Freud the ego – but he or she also remains closely identified with the mother. In both Freud and Lacan this bond with the mother is 'broken' during the 'resolution' of the Oedipus complex. Like Freud, Lacan sees this 'resolution' in terms of metaphorical castration – it is brought about by the intervention of the father as a 'third term', interrupting and disrupting the unity of the mother/child dyad. Lacan sees this process operating through the introduction of what he calls the 'Law of the father'. The law of fatherly interdiction, the name/*nom* or no/*non* of the father (*nom* and *non* are homonyms in French), introduces the threat of 'castration' and consequently breaks apart the mother/child dyad and causes the child's entry into the Symbolic. As the Symbolic is the state of language, Lacan's theory can be summarized as a rereading of Freud in terms of language. That is to say, Lacan's rereading of Freud considers that language is the thing that stands in for or represents what is absent or 'lacking'. One of the things the child 'lacks' in Lacan's Symbolic is the mother. The movement from the Imaginary to the Symbolic is one-way, irreversible – once the child, via the intervention of the father, has entered the Symbolic/language, the Imaginary (and by implication the mother) can only be accessed *through* the Symbolic. As a result of this, the bond between the child and the mother is weakened; whereas the bond between the father and language seems almost unbreakable.

However, the child still senses the mother's absence, still desires for a return to the pre-Oedipal state of bliss and unity. The Real is the space where this desire reaches 'fulfilment'. The Real is the space where we 'lack' nothing. However, as the Real is also non-verbal – and non-spatial, for that matter – like the Imaginary it can only be approached through the Symbolic (that is, through the medium of language). What is more, since the Symbolic/language is structured though lack, the Real, the space where there is no lack, will always be unobtainable. Entry into the 'adult' world of the Lacanian Symbolic/language can thus be seen as a metaphor for 'lost innocence'. Indeed, Cixous frequently returns to the story of Eve and the Garden of Eden in her critiques of the structures and underlying assumptions of patriarchy (see below). Through the Symbolic, through language, it can be argued that Lacan creates a prison for unconscious, non-verbal desires. Because the Imaginary and the Real can never be directly experienced, Lacan privileges the Symbolic – giving it the precedence over the other two terms.

What Cixous does in 'Sorties' is to question whether there might not be another way, whether a different system of relationships might be employed. This would be a system closer to the Imaginary and the Real, one that does not have to revolve around the concept of 'lack'. Though it is seemingly concerned with abstract issues, Cixous argues that this new system *could* exist and, crucially, that there would be far-reaching political and social consequences if it did. Cixous suggests that this different system can be achieved through a radical reappraisal of the relationship between the self and the non-self – between the self and the 'other'.

The murder of the m/other

'Sorties' begins with a question: 'Where is she?' (p. 63). The eye is then drawn to a list of words that cascade down the page like a pack of cards falling out of a hand:

Activity/passivity
Sun/Moon
Culture/Nature
Day/Night.   (p. 63)

Consciously or unconsciously connections are formed. Because of the way Western European languages are read, because of the system of collective cultural references that lurk beneath the surface of society, 'she' appears to be found in the terms on the right.

Consciously or unconsciously the terms on the left seem to take priority, appear to be More Important. This process carries on as Cixous continues her list: 'Father/Mother', 'Head/Heart', and so on (p. 63). Cixous laments the continual recurrence of 'the same metaphor' (p. 63). Throughout history, she observes, there is a certain process of thinking that 'has always worked through opposition' (p. 63). Cixous contends that this philosophical system of oppositions, which she calls 'Logocentrism' (p. 64), is hierarchical in nature and insidious in effect. It requires that 'woman' be the passive partner in all oppositions – that 'woman' not be allowed any control over her own destiny. In the patriarchal system Cixous is describing, 'woman', like the pre-Oedipal body of the mother in the Real, is something that is 'absent, hence desirable' (p. 67). 'Woman' is necessary to the system, but at the same time excluded from it. An example of the kind of hierarchical system Cixous is describing here can be found in the relationship between the Lacanian self and the other. Lacan's construction of the self, which first happens in what he calls the 'Mirror Stage', is reliant on the presence of an 'other' to reflect back an image of the self.[2] The relationship between the self and the other is constructed along the same lines as the relationship between the self and the image of the self someone sees in a mirror when viewing their reflection. As Lacan explains, on first perceiving its 'specular image' – whether this be in an actual or metaphorical mirror (such as the body of the mother) – the child undergoes '*an identification*' with this image, producing, Lacan says, an '*imago*' of the body that allows the child to distinguish between the I and the not-I, the self and the other (*Écrits*, pp. 2–3). Again, it needs to be stressed that this relationship between the self and the other is not reciprocal. The other might confirm the identity of the Lacanian self, but the Lacanian self denies the right to identity of the other. The other is appropriated, used and discarded. As Cixous herself puts it: the Lacanian self is created through the 'murder of the other' (*The Newly Born Woman*, p. 70).

Bringing the idea of 'woman' (the mother) and the idea of the 'other' together, one can see how the two are linked together in 'Sorties' (the term 'm/other' is often used to signal this connection). Both woman and the other are subject to or enslaved by what

Cixous calls 'the master/slave dialectic' (p. 70). Neither one of them is tolerated nor allowed to exist in their own right. It is perhaps inevitable that an occasional slippage occurs in Cixous's discussion of woman and the other in 'Sorties'. Here Cixous might be discussing the relationship *between* woman and the other, there she might be talking about woman *as* other. However, it is not so much the particular referents used at any one moment, but the system of relationships between these referents to which attention must be paid. Cixous contends that in any 'hierarchically organized relationship' (p. 71) the other (in whatever form it may take) is that which is appropriated, repressed, excluded and annihilated through the actions of the underlying oppositional system. However, she claims, by altering the relationship with this other it is possible that the system itself will also be changed:

> There have to be ways of relating that are completely different from the tradition ordained by the masculine economy. So, urgently and anxiously, I look for a scene in which a type of exchange would be produced that would be different, a kind of desire that wouldn't be in collusion with the old story of death. This desire would invent Love, it alone would not use the word love to cover up its opposite ... On the contrary, there would have to be a recognition of each other ... each would take the risk of the *other*, of difference, without feeling threatened by the existence of an otherness, rather, delighting to increase through the unknown that is there to discover, to respect, to favor, to cherish.   (p. 78)

Cixous finds that this different way of relating to the other can be expressed and explored through writing. Writing, she claims, is that 'somewhere else that can escape the infernal repetition' of the patriarchal system (p. 72). Because she is offering an alternative to the so-called 'masculine' economy of patriarchal discourse, Cixous refers to this different economy as 'feminine writing' – *écriture féminine*.

Qualifiers of sexual difference

There has been a certain amount of confusion and misunderstanding over the years surrounding the question of 'sexual difference' in

Cixous's work. As was indicated above, in the case of 'Sorties' this confusion has partly arisen because Cixous herself is not entirely consistent in her use of terminology. At times Cixous focuses on sex-specific experiences, such as motherhood (see below), elsewhere she strives to distance her argument from such so-called 'essentialist' notions of the body. In her defence, it is important to remember that Cixous's essay is very much caught up in the historical whirlwind of its time – the mid-1970s. The demands of polemic (even more in evidence in 'The Laugh of the Medusa') might therefore explain some of the inconsistencies in 'Sorties'. However, it is also worth noting that a general ambivalence towards 'meaning' is an essential feature of Cixous's vision of *écriture féminine* (see esp. Chapter 5). Patriarchy seeks to reduce all things to a singular, 'phallic' meaning. In *écriture féminine* multiple, or even contradictory, meanings and forms of expressions are sought after and valued. Therefore, when reading Cixous, particularly the Cixous of the 1970s, words such as 'masculine' and 'feminine' need to be thought of as extremely fluid concepts – their meaning constantly shifting, unstable and unresolved.

When Cixous uses the words 'masculine' and 'feminine' in 'Sorties' she is deploying them as what she calls '*qualifiers* of sexual difference' (p. 81). Cixous adds that she does this 'to avoid the confusion man/masculine, woman/feminine' (p. 81). Masculinity is not the sole preserve of men, she argues, nor is femininity the sole preserve of women. 'We have to be careful', she remarks, 'not to lapse smugly or blindly into an essentialist, ideological interpretation' of the differences between the sexes (p. 81). These differences, Cixous contends, cannot be decided 'on the basis of socially determined "sexes"', nor should they rely on notions of 'a "natural", anatomical determination of sexual difference-opposition' (p. 81). That is to say, though men and women *are* different, it matters very much *how* this difference is thought of and defined. Certain 'social' or 'anatomical' determinations of difference are used to reinforce and justify patriarchal systems of power and control. However, she claims, there are other ways in which sexual difference can be viewed and expressed.

Cixous's alternative approach to sexual difference can be seen in the way in which she 'deconstructs' Freud's theory of castration.

In Freud's theory the Oedipus complex is 'resolved' when the child, having seen the mother and the father naked, observes that the mother does not 'have' a penis. Unconsciously ascribing this to an act of 'castration' on the part of the father, the child feels threatened with the prospect of a similar 'castration' and thus switches its affections and 'allegiance' from the mother to the father. It has to be said that Cixous oversimplifies Freud's writing in 'Sorties', making him out to be even more dogmatic and insensitive than he might otherwise appear.[3] But Cixous is deliberately exaggerating certain 'truths' in order to make a more general point about the workings of patriarchal society. Unlike many of the people involved in the women's movement in the 1970s, who dismissed Freud's theories outright on account of his overtly patriarchal, occasionally misogynous world-view, Cixous writes elsewhere about how useful and inspirational his work can be – particularly Freud's writings on dreams and the unconscious (Cixous's own writing on the subject of dreams is discussed in Chapter 4).[4] In her 'Conversations' with the members of the Centre d'Etudes Féminines, Cixous explains her use of Freud in terms of an analogy. Just as no-one would expect 'feminists' (another term she distances herself from) not to use aeroplanes because they have 'been invented by men', neither should one ignore Freud's theories just because of the kind of man Freud himself had been:

> Freud focused attention on the unconscious in an extraordinary series of discoveries. Do we behave as if the unconscious doesn't exist? We live in a post-Freudian, Derridean age of electricity and the aeroplane. So let's do as modern people do, let's use the contemporary means of transport. We owe Freud the exploration of the unconscious.[5]

Inherent in Freud's theory (or at least in the deliberately reductive reading of his theory Cixous is engaged in) is the idea that everything will always return to the 'masculine', to the presence or absence of the penis. Observing the impossibility of adequately reconciling female sexuality with this theory of castration, Cixous argues that Freud drapes female sexuality in a veil of mystery and unknowing: 'the "dark continent" trick has been pulled on her: she has been kept at a distance from herself, she has been made to see (= not-see) woman on the basis of what man wants her to see, which is to say, almost nothing' (*The Newly Born Woman*, p. 68). Freud compared the secrets of feminine sexuality to what Western colonial eyes saw as the supposed mysterious and impenetrable depths of the continent of Africa. His point was that, for him, both were 'unexplorable', unknowable. Yet, by expressing himself in this manner he also highlights the underlying culture of oppression and denial implicit in his ideas about the nature of both the non-male and the non-white-European 'other'. Freud manages to roll colonialism and patriarchy into one – as a woman, Jewish, and 'French Algerian', Cixous is adversely affected by this in a number of ways.

Cixous observes that women 'have internalized this fear of the dark', adding that patriarchy has conditioned women to be frightened, even 'disgusted' at the thought of their own sexuality: 'Their bodies, which they haven't dared enjoy, have been colonized' (p. 68). She suggests that it doesn't have to be this way and offers a different approach to the question of sexual difference. Cixous rejects Freud's reliance on the visual, on what she calls his 'fantasized relation to anatomy', arguing instead for a 'difference' rooted in the sensual and sexual experiences of the body – a difference that 'becomes most clearly perceived on the level of *jouissance* ["pleasure"]' (p. 82).[6] Though her preference for a difference marked by *jouissance* might seem to perpetuate the spirit of oppositional differences – in that men and women's experience of sexual and other pleasures are not the same – in actuality a subtle change in the way the system of relations operates has taken place. Cixous effectively removes the hierarchical element present in the previously existing definition of sexual difference. As it is reliant on the fact of whether one has or does not have a penis Cixous calls this old approach to sexual difference 'phallocentrism' (p. 83). She remarks that even though it might *seem* biased in favour of men (the supposition being that the possession of the aforementioned object somehow conveys a mystical sense of superiority) it in fact oppresses 'everyone' (p. 83). Both sexes suffer the ill-effects of phallocentrism (even though one sex may be less aware of this fact than the other). The experience of 'loss' felt by men, she explains, 'is different from but just as serious as' the loss felt by women (p. 83).

Libidinal economies

Cixous argues that this new way of writing/relating to the other can only be achieved if one has a concept of self and of sex that is 'complex, mobile, open' – one in which 'the other sex' is accepted, freely and without hesitation, 'as a component' of the self (p. 84). 'It is only in this condition that we invent' (p. 84), Cixous proclaims, unconsciously echoing the comments made by Virginia Woolf in *A Room of One's Own* (1929).[7] Woolf's long essay is, like 'Sorties', concerned with the effect of gender on writing. Considering it to be 'fatal' for a writer to be 'man or woman pure and simple', Woolf puts forward the argument that a degree of 'collaboration' between the sexes 'has to take place in the mind . . . before the art of creation can be accomplished' (p. 94). Like Woolf, Cixous maintains 'that there is no *invention* possible . . . without there being in the inventing subject an abundance of the other, of variety' (*The Newly Born Woman*, p. 84). Not without controversy, Cixous chooses to refer to this state of openness to the other (sex) as an example of 'bisexuality' (pp. 84–5). Cixous's discussion of 'bisexuality' in 'Sorties', and other texts from around this time, has caused so much confusion over the years that she has now distanced herself entirely from the term (see *Rootprints*, pp. 50–1). 'Bisexuality' was a term much in vogue in psychoanalytical circles in the 1970s and it is important to note that Cixous is using the term within this frame of reference. That is to say, in this instance, 'bisexuality' is the psychic imprint made when one admits the 'presence' of both sexes in the mind – something akin to what Woolf, following Coleridge, called 'the androgynous mind' (*A Room of One's Own*, p. 95).

Although Cixous sees the potential in both men and women for this 'bisexuality', in most cases it will more often than not be located within women – men 'having been trained', she contends, 'to aim for glorious phallic monosexuality' (*The Newly Born Woman*, p. 85). It is this supposition that leads Cixous to make the claim that, 'today, writing is woman's' (p. 85). She does not intend this as 'a provocation', she explains, but merely as a recognition 'that woman admits there is an other' (p. 85). Cixous does not exclude men from this process, but claims that under the current system of sexual difference it is women who are much more likely have a close affinity with the other: 'It is much harder for man to let the other come through him' (p. 85). To illustrate this, Cixous takes note of the different ways in which women and men's bodies channel the experiences of *jouissance*/pleasure. Cixous claims that 'woman's' sexuality is infinitely plural, various and changing: it is 'endless body ... without principal "parts" ' (p. 87). She contrasts this with 'masculine sexuality', which, she says, is static and singular: 'gravitat[ing] around the penis' (p. 87).[8] In 'Coming to Writing' (written soon after 'Sorties'), Cixous is quite explicit in her belief that there are certain sex-specific experiences to which the other sex cannot gain access: 'all women feel in the dark or the light, what no man can experience in their place, the incisions, the births, the explosions in libido, the ruptures, the losses, the pleasures in our rhythms' (p. 56). However, though a man cannot experience these same sensations, or at least not to the degree of intensity a woman can, it is conceivable, Cixous argues, for a man to experience 'similar' or equivalent sensations (p. 56). This is conceivable, she concludes, whenever 'femininity is not forbidden', whenever a man, as she colourfully puts it, 'doesn't fantasize his sexuality around a faucet' (p. 56). Of course, as Cixous admits to Mireille Calle-Gruber, although she 'would like to', because she is a woman it is not possible for her to truly 'know' the sensations and experiences of 'masculine *jouissance*' (*Rootprints*, p. 53). One reason for this is that, whether it be 'feminine' or 'masculine', *jouissance* cannot be fully expressed in language – it operates on the fringes or even outside the space of the verbal. Therefore, *jouissance* cannot be fully 'communicated' from one sex to the other (although see Chapter 3 for how Cixous's writing for the theatre enables her to circumvent this problem). On the other hand, what *can* be expressed in language is the way in which one relates to *jouissance*/pleasure – specifically, whether one 'denies' oneself *jouissance*/pleasure, or not.

In a lecture entitled 'The Author in Truth' Cixous remarks that she has 'often' used the term 'libidinal economies' in her discussions of sexual difference.[9] With reference to the stories of Eve from Genesis and Percival from the Grail legends, Cixous explains that the different libidinal economies can be illustrated by the way in which one chooses to react in situations 'in which desire and prohibition coexist' (*Coming to Writing*, p. 149). In the case of Eve, Cixous compares her reaction to 'the word of the Law' (p. 150) when faced with the decision of whether or not to eat the fruit of the tree of knowledge, with the response of Abraham when he is commanded 'to sacrifice his son, the one he loves' (p. 151). In both situations, she contends, 'the law is incomprehensible' – there is no such thing as 'death' in the Garden of Eden and Abraham is given no reason whatsoever why his son must die (p. 151). Yet, while Eve chooses to disobey and to 'taste' the apple (to experience the pleasure of eating the apple), Abraham, in spite of the love he feels for his son, 'obeys absolutely, without question' (p. 151). The symbolism of food and of eating is important for Cixous in her discussion of Eve and the law. Cixous argues that the story of Eve can be reduced to a 'simple' dilemma: will one transgress, will one take pleasure in and be nourished by the unknown 'intimate inside of the fruit' (p. 149), or will one stay on the side of the law, hungry but content in the bliss of ignorance? This conflict between pleasure and prohibition also appears in Cixous's account of Percival's 'marvelous meal' at the court of the Fisher King (p. 149). During this meal, Percival observes 'a procession of servants' bearing 'splendid dishes into another room' (p. 153). Because he has been taught 'that in life one-does-not-ask-questions' (p. 153), Percival watches and says nothing. Nor does he intervene when a bloodied 'lance' (suggestive of castration) is carried back and forth in front of him 'many times' (p. 153). Percival remains silent throughout his meal. Bound by the conventions of the law – to which, in his mind, he remains true – Percival merely 'takes pleasure in all the excellent foods that are served' (p. 153). However, Cixous relates that, unbeknownst to him, the law is playing a trick on Percival, placing him in an impossible, irresolvable situation. Because of Percival's failure to speak out and question the events happening in front of him, it is claimed that he has failed to prevent the death of the Fisher King. Percival is condemned for his crime, yet, Cixous argues, the condemnation handed down by the law is unfair. Percival is bound by the conventions of the law not to ask questions. Although he obeys the law, he is nevertheless 'punished for not having done something he wasn't supposed to do' (p. 154). What one can see in both Eve and Percival's condemnations, Cixous claims, is the inherent 'absurdity' of the law (p. 154). On the one side there are the meaningless, nonsensical dictates of the law, on the other are the simple, innocent experiences of pleasure. Cixous claims that both Eve and Percival's stories are 'poetic' texts – texts in which the protagonist is able to experience 'pleasure' in spite of the discourse of 'antipleasure' that the law represents (p. 154). Cixous explains that in the case of the latter, Percival is a creature of 'innocence' and 'pleasure': 'While the law weaves its web, Percival is extremely happy, he eats enjoyable things, enjoys himself as much as he can' (p. 154).[10] The fact that Percival gives himself freely and entirely to the experience of pleasure therefore places him in a similar position to that of Eve. As Cixous concludes, it is 'the individual's responses to this strange, antagonistic relationship' between pleasure and the law, which 'inscribe – whether we are men or women – different paths through life' (pp. 154–5).

Cixous believes that in the stories of Eve and Percival one can see that 'the fate of the *so-called feminine economy* is at stake' (p. 149). Cixous is tentative about the word 'feminine', because, as the story of Percival shows, 'this economy is not the endowment solely of women' (p. 149). She explains that she uses the words ' "feminine" and "masculine" because we are born into language, and because I cannot do otherwise than to find myself preceded by words' (p. 150). Cixous argues that it would make no difference if these words were replaced by 'synonyms' – such synonyms 'would become as closed, as immobile and petrifying, as the words "masculine" and "feminine" ' have become today (p. 150). All that one can do, she remarks, is to play with these words to stretch their meaning and signification as far as it will go. Therefore, although she must use the words 'feminine' and 'masculine', she will turn them inside out, upside down, bend them, fold them and 'shake them all the time, like apple trees' (p. 150).

Writing the body

Difference is inscribed in many forms. Cixous suggests in 'Sorties' that one can also see 'difference come through in writing . . . in the manner of spending, of valorizing the appropriated' (p. 86). The concept of the gift, like *jouissance*, can be thought of in terms of 'masculine' and 'feminine' economies. In his highly influential study of this subject, *The Gift: The Form and Reason for Exchange in Archaic Societies* (1950; trans. 1990), the social anthropologist Marcel Mauss introduces a series of interrelated pre-industrial systems of exchange, the most famous of which is the North American potlatch. In the potlatch, says Mauss, there are three distinct obligations: 'to give, to receive, to reciprocate'.[11] To fail to accept any one of these obligations is considered a great insult. Since each reciprocation becomes in its own way another gift, the cycle of giving-and-receiving-and-reciprocating is endless and unbroken. 'It is possible to extend these observations to our own societies', Mauss proposes: 'A considerable part of our morality and our lives themselves are still permeated with this same atmosphere of the gift ... The unreciprocated gift still makes the person who has accepted it inferior, particularly when it has been accepted with no thought of returning it' (p. 67). Troubled by what she calls in 'Medusa' the 'gift-that-takes' (p. 292), Cixous wonders if there is any way for 'woman to escape this law of return' (*The Newly Born Woman*, p. 87). As she shows in a number of texts, including 'Coming to Writing', the experience of motherhood offers a way out of this self-perpetuating, circular economy of the 'masculine' gift. Motherhood is a 'gift' one 'gives' to the other.[12]

Cixous considers that motherhood represents what is possibly the most intense and complete relationship with the other that can be had. As she remarks in 'The Author in Truth', the potential or actual experience of being pregnant gives women a unique perspective on the other: 'women ... have an experience of the inside, an experience of the capacity for other, and experience of nonnegative change brought about by the other, of positive receptivity' (p. 155). Drawing on her own personal experience of motherhood, in 'Sorties' Cixous puts forward a strong argument for the potential of pregnancy to inspire a radical reappraisal of one's relations with the other, the 'feminine' body and writing:

> It is not only a question of the feminine body's extra resource, this specific power to produce some thing living of which her flesh is the locus, not only a question of a transformation of rhythms, exchanges, of relationship to space, of the whole perceptive system, but also of the irreplaceable experience of those moments of stress, of

> the body's crises, of that work that goes on peacefully for a long time
> only to burst out in that surpassing moment, the time of childbirth
> ... It is also the experience of a 'bond' with the other, all that comes
> through in the metaphor of bringing into the world. How could a
> woman, who has experienced the not-me within me, not have a
> particular relationship to the written?   (p. 90)

The 'bond' Cixous speaks of here is not the bond of reciprocation
and return outlined by Mauss. On the contrary, she says, the (sex-
specific) experiences of pregnancy and childbirth demonstrate that
there exists 'a bond between woman's libidinal economy – her *jouissance*, the feminine Imaginary – and her way of self-constituting a
subjectivity that splits apart without regret' (p. 90). As with pregnancy, Cixous likens the acceptance of the presence of the other
in *écriture féminine* to a kind of (positive, pleasurable) 'possession'
(p. 86). Cixous says that once she has embarked on the process
of writing, 'all those that we don't know we can be write themselves
from me' (p. 100). To allow for the presence of these others, she
argues, it is necessary to risk losing the self, to immerse oneself
fully, willingly, possibly irrevocably and without 'return', into 'the
unknown' (see Chapters 3 and 4). Cixous suggests in 'Coming to
Writing' that it is only at this point, when the body and the other
are at their closest point of contact, when 'flesh lets strangeness
come through', that writing will 'well up, surge forth, from the
throats of your unknown inhabitants' (pp. 38–9). Though the experience of maternity is largely sex-specific, Cixous nevertheless
argues in 'Sorties' that men can and should be involved. Cixous
argues that the roles played by parents 'must also be rethought',
to give the child the freedom necessary to be themself, to be other:
'It will be the task of woman and man to make the old relationship
and all its consequences out-of-date; to think the *launching* of a new
subject, into life, with defamiliarization' (p. 89).

The writing that this process 'gives birth to' is a writing that is
able to take a step or two back from the rigidity and spiritual emptiness of the Symbolic. Cixous comments that this other writing,
écriture féminine, draws close to and taps into the pre-verbal spaces
of the unconscious and the instinctual drives – it listens to and
allows one 'to hear what-comes-before-language reverberating'
(p. 88). It is Cixous's belief that such writing exceeds boundaries

and 'overflows' in a way that is 'vertiginous' and 'intoxicating' at one and the same time (p. 91).[13] Cixous compares the slight but enjoyable anxiety that comes from the sensation of losing control in *écriture féminine* to the sickening 'torture' a woman 'exposes' herself to when she is asked to give a public speech (p. 92). She argues that women 'are not culturally accustomed to speaking' (p. 92). In oratory, Cixous contends, one does not have the time nor the leeway to let the 'feminine' express itself to the full. Oratory is too certain: it makes no allowance for 'uneasiness' and 'questioning'; it restricts the possibility of 'waste', 'superabundance' and 'uselessness' – all of which, she argues, women 'like' and 'need' (p. 93). This is one of the reasons why Cixous privileges writing. Unlike speech, she argues, writing can take place in its own time, on its own terms. Writing will not be inhibited by the disapproving gaze of an audience. Cixous claims that she writes for no-one but herself (see *Rootprints*, p. 100). Writing, she says, is a space experimentation, a space where one can let 'the tongue try itself out' (*The Newly Born Woman*, p. 93). Writing, when looked at from the point of view Cixous is promoting, is a space of liberation.

Cixous sees this liberation coming about through a return to and rediscovery of the body. As was discussed above, she argues that women have been made to feel ashamed of their bodies: 'to lash them in stupid modesty' (p. 94). To counter this, Cixous contends, 'Woman must write her body' (p. 94). What this means, she explains, is that women must pay attention to all the non-verbal, unconscious, instinctual drives and sensations of their bodies – they must accent language with the patterns, reverberations and echoes emerging from these states. Cixous contends that 'woman is more body than man is' (p. 95). However, the word 'woman' in 'Sorties' is not only a reference to anatomical or biological sex, it is also a signifier of a different approach to the other (and to subjectivity and writing). For instance, soon after this passage Cixous comments (with a noticeable shift from the plural to the singular) that Shakespeare and Kleist can be thought of as examples of 'men who are capable of becoming woman' (p. 98). It is because of such writers, Cixous remarks, that she herself is now able to write. She sees in Shakespeare and Kleist examples of men who have had the courage to buck the trend, to defy convention.

Shakespeare and Kleist, she argues, found a way to circumvent and escape from the system: 'For the huge machine that tricks and repeats its "truth" for all these centuries has had its failures ... There have been poets who let something different from tradition get through at any price – men able to love love; therefore, to love others, to want them' (p. 98).

The physicality of writing matters. Like others, such as Derrida, Cixous makes play with the fact that '*écriture*' can mean both 'writing' and 'handwriting'. Cixous emphasizes the speed in which 'feminine' texts must be written – the flow of the hand, the touch of the fingers, the pulse of the blood in the arm.[14] By means of letting go and allowing the body to 'make itself heard', *écriture féminine* taps into what Cixous refers to as 'the huge resources of the unconscious' (p. 97). The practice of *écriture féminine* results in a variety of disruptive meanings being brought to bear on seemingly 'stable' texts. This introduction of instability is radical and creative. Cixous argues that women must do away with the controlling devices of phallic/Symbolic discourse: 'syntax', 'explanation', 'interpretation' and 'localization' (p. 96). Playing on the double sense of the verb '*voler*' ('to fly/steal'), she remarks that it is 'woman's gesture' to break into language and appropriate it for herself – to possess it, to transform it: 'to steal into language to make it fly' (p. 95). In light of this, one might say that *écriture féminine* acts like a kind of computer virus that infects and rewrites the Symbolic – the governing code/ discourse of patriarchy. As Cixous remarks, the process is 'slow' and 'difficult', but it is inexorable: an 'absolutely unstoppable, painful rising that ... finally tears open, wets and spreads apart what is dull and thick, the stolid, the volumes' (p. 88). Once language has been taken over by such a writing, once it has become 'woman's', everything changes. As Cixous exultantly proclaims in one of the most widely quoted sentences of her essay: 'Now, I-woman am going to blow up the Law: a possible and inescapable explosion from now on; let it happen, right now, in language' (p. 95).

Chapter 3

Fiction and theatre

But in the domain of women nothing can be theorized ... The
only thing one can say is that writing can, not tell or theorize it,
but play with it or sing it.

('From the Scene of the Unconscious ...', pp. 11–12)

Hélène Cixous's fiction and theatrical writing operates in a space
somewhere between poetic form and philosophical thought. Her
writing has always played with convention: adopting non-standard
(non-'masculine') approaches to style, characterization and plot
that disorientate, delight and challenge the reader/audience. One
can observe in Cixous's fiction and theatrical writing many of
the ideas that underlie *écriture féminine* being put into practice. The
changes and developments that take place in these texts reveal a
good deal about how *écriture féminine* might come to terms with such
questions as subjectivity and identity, subject matter, style and
genre. It is also the contention of this present chapter that Cixous's
fiction and theatrical writing acts as a kind of 'test bed' for the ideas
put forward in her 'theoretical' writing – an exercise in empirical
experimentation which feeds into her 'theory' of *écriture féminine*.

Beginnings

Given the great emphasis that is laid in 'Sorties' and other texts
on the need to open writing up to the other, to allow the other to
speak as other, Cixous's early texts can come as something of a
surprise. With *Inside*, Cixous's first work of fiction, the reader is distanced from the text by the over-emphasis on the 'character' of
the 'I' ('character', because Cixous tends to avoid conventional

characters in her fiction – see below).[1] The other (whether it be the figure of the 'father', the 'mother', the 'brother', and so on) is filtered through the 'I', leaving the reader wholly reliant on what is by any reckoning a highly subjective version of events. At first, this appears to run contrary to the new relation to the other Cixous describes and advocates in her writing on *écriture féminine*. However, it is important to note that *Inside* was written before Cixous fully developed her 'theory' of *écriture féminine* – all of her important writings on *écriture féminine* post-date *Inside* by at least half a decade. In addition to this, as Cixous explains in her 'Conversations' with the members of the Centre d'Etudes Féminines, it is not possible to create a writing that is open to the other without first understanding the nature of the subject who will be creating this writing:

> The inaugural gesture of writing is always in a necessary relation to narcissism. When one begins to write, one is constantly reminding oneself of the fact: 'I write' ... It takes time for 'I' to get used to 'I'. Time for the 'I' to be sure 'I' exists. Only then is there room for the other.   (p. 153)

Whether Cixous deliberately sets out with this intention when she writes *Inside*, or whether she later reads this intention back into her early work, is not important. What matters is that *Inside* and the other early texts are (consciously or unconsciously) written within this process of reaching the other through a greater awareness of the 'I'.

Inside charts the emergence of the 'I' in a text that is densely encoded with autobiographical allusions (although, as Cixous states in her 'Inter Views' with Mireille Calle-Gruber, her writing should never be thought of as directly or fully participating in the genre of autobiography itself – see below and *Rootprints*, p. 87). *Inside* explores some of the necessary pre-conditions of *écriture féminine*. It lays the ground. For instance, in one of the central images of the fiction a disembodied mouth appears and disappears, its place being taken by an equally disembodied hand (see *Inside*, pp. 63–5). In the imagery of this passage one can see a parallel with Cixous's descriptions of 'voice' and (hand)writing in 'Sorties' – with the idea that woman's voice is expressed and heard most clearly in her (hand)writing. The image is also suggestive of the link between eating and pleasure discussed in 'The Author in Truth'. Anticipating the openness and fluidity of Cixous's later 'libidinal economies', together with her wariness of patriarchal notions of sexual difference, the gender of the 'I' in *Inside* is shifting and unstable: 'sex was determined independently of anatomical and physiological requirements' (p. 79). It is worth noting how strongly death figures in *Inside*. Death is a central concern of Cixous's entire writing project – particularly her vision of *écriture féminine*. *Inside* follows the struggle as the 'I' strives to come to terms with the death of the father, both as a child and then, twenty years later, as an adult. Through exploring the themes of death and 'lack', the 'I' constructs an identity 'inside' or 'within' language (the French title, *Dedans*, can also be translated as *Within*). Death is always the starting point. As Cixous recounts in 'From the Scene of the Unconscious . . .', it is her belief 'that one can only begin to advance along the path of discovery . . . from the point of mourning' (p. 5). Only when all has been lost will the writer be able to appreciate and hold on to whatever is found or 'regained' (p. 4). It is thus necessary, Cixous adds, for a writer 'to do the apprenticeship of Mortality' (p. 5). The role of the mother in this process has strong affinities with the role of the mother (and maternity) in the emergence of the writing subject in *écriture féminine*. Though it is the father who is responsible for giving the 'I' language, after the father has died it is the mother who helps form the social self of the 'I' within language. Likewise, though the adult 'I' takes a number of (male) lovers in the second section of the fiction (supposedly, the 'I' claims, as 'substitutes' for the father), the mother still figures significantly as the 'I' develops a sense of self that turns from death to love. Near the close of the fiction, when the death of the father has been accepted and the 'I' luxuriates in the new, transcendent possibilities of language, the spectral presence of the (living) mother can be found. The figure of the father may be in the foreground, but the mother is an equally significant 'character'. As Cixous relates in 'From the Scene of the Unconscious . . .': 'the mother? She is music, she is there, behind, the force that breathes' (p. 4).

Cixous uses a number of 'experimental' forms of writing in *Inside*, improvising with such things as the punctuation, textual spacing, structure and characterization of the fiction. However, on the whole, *Inside* remains largely 'traditional' in its form; at least, that is, in comparison with Cixous's other early works of fiction. The narrative of her third fiction, *Le Troisième Corps* (*The Third Body*), follows Cixous's unnamed female narrator as she unravels and analyses the significance of her relationships with her dead father and her current lover (to whom she gives the name 'T.t.').[2] As with *Inside*, there are numerous autobiographical and psychoanalytical allusions woven into the text of *The Third Body*. Perhaps the most interesting of these, in terms of how it relates to Cixous's later thoughts on *écriture féminine*, is the way in which the 'third body' of the title appears to take shape as a form of 'feminine' writing. Meditating on the effects of sexual difference, perhaps while making love, perhaps while dreaming about making love (the text is deliberately ambiguous on such points), the narrator reports: 'At the intersection of our tongues there comes to us a third body, at a place where there is no law' (p. 70). 'Tongues' is significant here. The French *la langue* can refer to either a part of the body or to language – the word tongue is less commonly used in this second sense in English (although it is seen in the expression 'mother tongue'). At this libidinal 'intersection' of language and the body, the 'law' of the father (the 'law' of phallocentric discourse) gives way to a new system of relating, one that is 'feminine' in its indecisiveness, plurality and *jouissance*: 'inside the flesh is the singular feminine common noun of our limitless existence; set down in the cavity, moistened, stretched out, eyes closed, I let whoever materializes do what he/she will, to the point where masculine and feminine can no longer be distinguished' (p. 75). Flesh becomes text in the fiction's *dénouement* when the narrator and T.t. begin to write (he with the voice, she with the hand), creating a book that joins the narrator's 'right' and T.t.'s 'left' together in the 'same third body' (p. 156).

Alongside this 'third body' of writing, Cixous employs a variety of innovative systems of reference and narrative techniques in her work of fiction. Some of these innovations are more successful than others, but all, to some extent, open up the text to the presence of the other, or to otherness. For instance, Cixous includes words from other languages, such as the English 'knuckle', 'knock' and 'suckle' (p. 110). The narrator also expresses her thoughts in terms of numerology (see p. 9) and the mathematical language of algebra (see pp. 100–3). Even emptiness has meaning in *The Third Body*. Cixous always places great emphasis on the signifying potential of blank spaces or pages in her texts (see Chapter 6). At one point in *The Third Body*, the text is reduced to an extremely eloquent 'blank space' that silently yet evocatively continues the themes of absence, forgetting and the unspoken that had been occupying the narrator in the preceding paragraph (see pp. 98–9). There is also a variety of plays at the level of the signifier. It is perhaps no coincidence that *The Third Body* was published in 1970, the same year as Roland Barthes's *S/Z* (his virtuosic dissection of Balzac's story 'Sarrasine').[3] Like Barthes, Cixous plays upon the possibilities offered by the dual nature of the consonant 's'. The narrator mentions a 'lizard' (in French, '*lézard*'), the English word 'cheese' (also given in the text, in parentheses, as 'Tchi:z'), its German equivalent, '*Käse*', and the name 'Zöe' (pp. 113–4). When pronounced, all these words contain a 'z' sound. For several pages after this, any signifier with an 's' that is pronounced as a 'z' is spelled as it sounds (see *Le Troisième Corps*, pp. 164–6).[4] The final significance of the play on s/z becomes apparent later in the narrative, when the narrator recalls 'the first riddle' posed by her father (*The Third Body*, p. 143). As she relates, 'I had to answer this question: "What contains all the vowels and is split by a consonant with a double meaning?"' (p. 144). The answer to this question is 'bird' (in French '*oiseau*' – pronounced 'wazo'). The delight felt by the narrator as she accidentally stumbles on this solution (she is dreaming of a bird and speaks aloud) brings her joyful praise from her father. It is a key moment.

Other plays on the signifier are achieved with poetic transformations. Of course, as was mentioned in Chapter 1, most of these puns, alliterations and neologisms cannot cross over completely into another language. For instance, T.t.'s name is changed into '*Tôt*' (Early), as well as '*T.(ou)t*.', which can be read literally as 'T. (or) t.', but can also be construed to mean '*Tout*' (all or everything) (see pp. 149–50). In addition to these plays on signifiers, Cixous also weaves allusions to, quotations from and summaries of texts by other writers into *The Third Body*.[5] Three texts in particular run through the fiction, threaded in and out of the writing so that the boundaries between their narratives and the life of the narrator become porous and opaque: Wilhelm Jensen's *Gradiva* and two stories by Kleist ('The Earthquake in Chile' and 'The Marquise of O—').[6] Significantly, Cixous's narrator chooses to read Jensen's out-of-print original, rather than Freud's more well-known, more widely available psychoanalytical study of Jensen's novel.[7] By doing this, she manages both to tap into and to distance herself from the vogue for psychoanalysis running through intellectual Paris at the time *The Third Body* was written. Although Kleist is a better, more interesting writer than Jensen, his work was still not what one might call 'famous'. It is therefore important to make note of the fact that Cixous often takes her 'examples' or inspirations from writers who are not widely known. Her motivation is partly personal (a desire to share the joy she experiences when she reads these writers with others), but it is also political. The act of giving voice to 'non-canonical' writers and texts assists Cixous in her task of setting up an alternative, non-exclusive space of writing.[8]

Cixous's inclusion of these texts by other writers in her fictions takes place on a poetic rather than a critical level. That is to say, Cixous does not interpret or comment on the texts (as she does in her writing in other genres), but uses the themes and motifs she finds in them (hidden names and identities, fathers and maternity) as an artist might use the colours arranged on a palette, or the images collected for a collage – to bring light, shading, texture and complexity to the overall work. In the fiction previous to *The Third Body*, *Les Commencements* (*The Beginnings*), Cixous works in a similar fashion with a painting of St George and the dragon by the fifteenth-century Florentine artist Uccello.[9] She continues this practice in future works. For instance, Cixous's 1973 fiction, *Portrait du soleil* (*Portrait of the sun*),[10] and her 1976 play, *Portrait de Dora* (*Portrait of Dora*),[11] are both reworkings of and meditations upon Freud's first published case study.[12] Along with Freud, Kafka is a particularly common reference in Cixous's early writing. Her 1975 text, *Un K. incompréhensible: Pierre Goldman*, is a reworking of Kafka's *The Trial* written in order to highlight the case of a contemporary 'miscarriage of justice'.[13] Her 1982 fiction, *Limonade tout était si infini* (*Lemonade everything was so infinite*), takes its title and its narrative from one of Kafka's last pieces of writing: the handwritten notes he communicated with once he could no longer speak.[14] Another fiction, *Préparatifs de noces au-delà de l'abîme* (*Preparations for Marriage Beyond the Abyss*), evokes the title of one of Kafka's short stories: 'Wedding Preparations in the Country'.[15]

The experiments with form Cixous undertakes in *Inside* and, to a greater extent, in *The Third Body*, are also continued in later texts. *Partie* (*Part*) is printed so that it can be read from either end, with the two halves of the fiction meeting in the middle.[16] *Tombe* (*Tomb*) opens with a list of 33 numbered statements or propositions.[17] As with many of Cixous's fictions (and other works), paragraphs end with a comma, or no punctuation point at all. Single words and phrases appear isolated from the text, often in italics. Cixous also plays with the typesetting of the text in *Tombe*, setting the words 'a squirrel', for instance, thus (p. 78):

‘ ‘ ‘ ‘ ‘ ‘

! Un écureuil !

‘ ‘ ‘ ‘ ‘ ‘

Or, as in this other example, when she begins to make a list of the things that she loves (p. 87):

la peur   l'amour   la vérité   le présent   la présence

et   et   et   et   et

[fear   love   truth   present   presence

and   and   and   and   and]

In *Neutre* (*Neutral*), these innovations and experiments are carried to the extreme.[18] Though it is called a 'novel' ('roman') on the cover, *Neutre* is in fact a blend of genres: fiction, drama, poetry, psychology, philosophy. Following its six epigrams (pp. 6–15),[19] *Neutre* assumes the role of a play, giving a list of its 'JOUEURS, PIECES ET REVENANTS [PLAYERS, PIECES AND GHOSTS]' (p. 17). Cixous also engages in parodies of contemporary literary criticism (see, for example, pp. 165–6) and dictionaries (see p. 30). Ellipses are frequently employed. Sometimes these replace part of a word (see pp. 20, 23, 66) or an item in a list (see p. 28), but most often Cixous uses them to break up the narrative – inserting points of uncertainty, suggesting the possibility that both the spoken and the unspoken can be 'heard'. Words are also crossed through (see pp. 68, 73, 92), printed upside down (see p. 108) and replaced with long lines of dots (see pp. 93, 104). Cixous even plays with the words in her quotations, as in this example taken from Milton's *Samson Agonistes* (in English in the original text):

O darK dark dark amid the blaze of noon
O   a   a   a   a   oo   (p. 34)

Note the capital letter at the end of 'darK' – another allusion to Kafka's Joseph K, perhaps, or to the family, Herr and Frau K, who were involved in Freud's 'Dora' case?

On their own, it cannot be said that these various textual experiments constitute a 'feminine' approach to writing. However, as with the exploration of the 'I' in the early fiction, Cixous's experimentation with content and form during this period can be seen as an important step on the way towards an *écriture féminine*. In these early texts, Cixous takes the conventions of literature (genre, narrative, grammar, punctuation, syntax, the layout of the text on a page, and so on) and stretches them to see how far they can go. She is, at times, testing to destruction. These texts are written with the intention of resisting the impulse towards a single interpretation, but sometimes (especially in the case of *Neutre*) Cixous dismantles the forms of writing to such a degree that one begins to wonder if *any* interpretation is possible. That said, though they may present the reader with more than a few headaches (both figuratively and literally), in the long view these innovations and experiments can be seen as radical but much needed movements away from the past and from what has come before. If it is necessary to fully understand and appreciate the 'I' before moving on to a writing of the other, so is it necessary to understand the space in which this writing will take place. Sometimes one can only understand things by taking them apart. Sometimes there are one or two pieces left over when one tries to put everything back together again.

Metamorphosis

In the mid-1970s a shift occurs in Cixous's fiction and the accent moves from the figure of the father, and falls instead (albeit obliquely) on the figure of the mother and the 'feminine'. As was mentioned in Chapter 1, this is the period of Cixous's association with the MLF (Mouvement de Libération des Femmes). It also coincides with the time when Cixous chooses to publish her work through Antoinette Fouque's Des femmes publishing label. One of the key works of this period is Cixous's 1977 fiction *Angst* – the first of her fictions (if one does not count the bilingual *Vivre l'orange/To Live the Orange*) to be translated into English.[20] *Angst* is extremely interesting in terms of the development of *écriture féminine*. It carries the themes of loss and separation found in the early texts to an alto- gether higher degree of intensity. The pain experienced in *Angst* is raw and, at times, almost unbearable. The opening sentences of the text set the tone for what is to come: 'The worst is upon me. This is it: the scene of the Great Suffering' (p. 7). Although it is not an easy book to read (on an emotional level), from the outset there is also a sense of progress in *Angst*, a sense that difficult questions and issues are being worked through and resolved. There are many scenes of abandonment and betrayal. All of these appear to relate back to the feeling of being 'outside' that overwhelms the narrator the first time her mother leaves her alone: 'My mother puts me down on the ground. The room closes in. "Wait there for me. I'll be back straightaway." My mother goes out. The ground closes in. I am outside. When *I* am not there *you* die. Betrayed. Everything starts to die' (p. 8).

Angst is very much a threshold text. Death remains a potent force in *Angst*, but it also marks the crossing point where Cixous's writing begins to turn towards an exploration of the question of love. In a postscript to the French edition (not included in the English trans- lation), Cixous looks back on the writing that has led to *Angst* and comments: 'dix ans pour faire un pas, le premier après dieu la mort, dix ans pour arracher l'amour à la contemplation de dieu la folle. Dix livres à vouloir en finir avec la mort [ten years to take a step, the first after god the dead, ten years to draw out love from the contemplation of god the fool. Ten books to want to finish it with death]' (French text, p. 281). In *Angst*, the self is (re)born through a conscious recognition of her own mortality (see English text, p. 29). Writing is the medium through which one can connect with death. Cixous's narrator compares the act of writing to a 'duel' that one 'is

fighting against death' (p. 116). However, she argues, it is impera-
tive that if one wishes to write, one must never win this duel: 'if the
battle that binds them together were to end in your victory, in
death's defeat – you would never lift your pen' (p. 116). As will be
discussed later (see below, and Chapter 4), this non-resolvable state
of uncertainty is something that is of immense appeal to Cixous.
For her, writing would die if it was forced into the circumstance
where closure or finality becomes inevitable. As the narrator of
Angst remarks: 'It is a question of an end without ending. A death
that is not over, that I am still savouring today' (p. 188). Throughout *Angst*, the narrator is struggling to express 'the violent intensity of a happiness being played out on the borders of death and
eternity' (p. 144). Early on in the fiction, she describes her birth
as 'a serious experiment in language' (p. 19). Soon afterwards,
in a passage that strongly resonates with the call for a revolution-in-
language Cixous makes in 'Sorties', the narrator advises: 'If there
is no earth, invent it, if the earth doesn't go fast enough, leave it
behind, take off, if there's no road, make one, invent it with feet,
hands, arms, passions, necessity' (p. 54). There is a strong link
forged between language and the body, a feeling that there is 'no
dividing line between bodies and words' (p. 112). There is also a
connection with Cixous's descriptions of the non-verbal space of the
'feminine' Imaginary: 'No ordinary language was spoken; nothing
can be explained. The things that happened were not expressed in
words' (p. 190).

Angst witnesses the emergence of a new approach to the self and
its others, a new way of relating to both the 'I' and that which is
'outside'. The self intends to make room for the other with a truly
radical act of letting go. Having intently and repeatedly explored
the many facets of the 'inside' of the 'I', Cixous's narrator feels that
she now has reached the point where 'the next step' can be taken
(p. 190). Stepping 'outside', the narrator intends to let go of all
sense of familiarity: 'Cut yourself off absolutely. Become alien.
Feel the other's powerful presence inside you, stronger than you,
and cease to be anyone but the other' (p. 191). This is a journey
into a spiritual wilderness, a washing away of all that has been
before. Cixous's narrator compares her isolation during this process
to the 'forty days and forty nights' of the Flood (p. 168). By the final

paragraph of the text the narrator, purged, has become a space of potentiality: 'I got rid of god. I finally threw up love. Nothing left but the bared soul. How clean I was, how purified, wrung dry ... I didn't have to love any-body. It was love loving; whom I love' (p. 219). At the end of *Angst* the way is left open for the entry of the other. However, there is also the possibility that this 'purgation' might result in an impasse or dead end. Fortuitously, it is at this moment that the writing of Clarice Lispector appears on the scene. The importance of Cixous's 'discovery' of Lispector's writing cannot be overstated. It would be interesting to speculate how Cixous's fiction might have developed had she not encountered Clarice Lispector's work, so important does this become to Cixous in the 1980s. Cixous's critical writing on Lispector will be discussed later (see Chapter 5). What is significant at present is the effect Lispector's writing has on Cixous's own fictional practice.

The voice of the other

In 'From the Scene of the Unconscious ...' Cixous recalls the moment when, through a chance encounter, she first saw the writing of Clarice Lispector:

> Two people came to speak to me in 1977 of a writer named Clarice Lispector ... I glanced at some fragments of texts, I was dazzled, I took it to be a wonderful accident. And then as I went on in the text I discovered an immense writer, the equivalent for me of Kafka, with something more: this was a woman, writing as a woman. I discovered Kafka and it was a woman. This was a time when I had written a lot and had read a lot and I was feeling a little lonely in literature. And then out of the blue I met this woman. It was unexpected.   (p. 10)

One of Cixous's most visible and powerful responses to this discovery was the writing of *Vivre l'orange/To Live the Orange*. *Vivre l'orange* is a short, intensely poetic text – part tribute, part hymn, part joyful outpouring of words, sounds, images, ideas. Cixous makes it plain quite early on in the text that Lispector has rescued her as a writer, rescued her writing, breathed new life into both Cixous the author and her work. Lispector's writing arrives 'with an angel's footsteps' at the time when Cixous's 'writing-being was grieving for being so lonely' (p. 10). As Cixous recounts: 'I wandered ten glacial years in over-published solitude, without seeing a single human woman's face, the sun had retired, it was mortally cold, the truth had set, I took the last book before death, and behold, it was Clarice, the writing' (p. 48). The gratitude and the love Cixous feels for Lispector infuses every page of *Vivre l'orange* with an almost religious fervour. What Lispector's writing gives to Cixous is described in *Vivre l'orange* as the double gift of 'the woman I had loved being' and the pleasure of being able to know once more 'the orange's goodness, the fruit's fullness' (p. 14). The orange of *Vivre l'orange* is many things. Like Eve's apple, it operates as a metaphor for the joy of life and the joy of living.[21] The orange is associated with a return to the experiences of childhood (see p. 14). It also opens the way for a journey to what Cixous calls 'the source', 'the birth-voice' (p. 16). The 'source' Cixous speaks of here is recognizable as the pre-Symbolic space of the 'feminine' Imaginary she describes in essays such as 'Sorties' and 'Coming to Writing'. As she had indicated in these essays, this pre-Symbolic 'source' has the power to make 'all voyages possible' (*Vivre l'orange*, p. 20). One might say that Cixous finds in Lispector the very precedents and examples she has been seeking all these years in the course of her own quest to create an *écriture féminine*. As was argued above, *écriture féminine* can be thought of as a writing of the other, a writing that makes room for and values the other *as other*. Cixous argues that Lispector possesses the necessary 'innocence' and 'courage' to bring this new way of relating to/with the other into being. Lispector is able to go 'to the foreign parts of the self' and to return, she says, 'almost without self, without denying the going' (p. 28). In contrast, despite the good intentions expressed at the close of *Angst*, at this stage of her own writing Cixous believes that she has not yet been able to totally commit herself to this journey. Lispector's gift of the orange, she feels, will inspire her to do so.

Another problem highlighted in *Vivre l'orange* is the position of 'infinite delicateness' the writer is placed in when trying to give life to the other-that-is-loved within language (p. 8). To preserve the uniqueness, the otherness of the other, the writer must learn how 'to watch over and save, not to catch', she must resist the impulse 'to seize and mean' and instead adopt a position that will 'reflect and protect the things that are ever as delicate as the newly-born' (p. 8). The position of the writer in relation to the loved other is one of the primary concerns of Cixous's 1983 fiction, *Le Livre de Promethea* (*The Book of Promethea*).[22]

Promethea opens with an admission: 'I am a little afraid of this book. Because it is a book of love' (p. 3). However, *Promethea* is not just a book about loving, or about being in love, it is also a book about *being loved*. The narrator admits to her competence at loving, and at expressing her love: 'But to be loved, that is true greatness. Being loved, letting oneself be loved, entering the magic and dreadful circle of generosity, receiving gifts, finding the right thank-you's, that is love's real work' (p. 20). Note how in *Promethea* Cixous is still reworking and reconfiguring the economy of the gift. Mauss's obligation to 'give, receive, reciprocate' has become a 'magic and dreadful circle of generosity' ('dreadful' is not necessarily a negative word here – it can be taken to mean 'awe-inspiring'). Describing Promethea, the object and source of love (the receiver and the giver of love), as her 'heroine', Cixous's narrator reflects that 'the question of writing is my adversary' (p. 14). Writing is her adversary because she is anxious to avoid a position of mastery or over-determination in her approach to the creation of what is, after all, Promethea's book.[23] In order to facilitate a writing position that can both 'reflect and protect' Promethea, Cixous splits her writing self in two (just as she splits the text of *Vivre l'orange* into 'English' and 'French'). Consequently, there are not one, but two narrators in *Promethea*: 'I' and 'H'.[24] Cixous's narrator remarks that because she has divided herself into I and H, it is possible for her 'to slip continually from one to the other' (p. 12), releasing herself from the chains of 'autobiography' – a form of writing that she considers to be 'jealous' and 'deceitful' (p. 19). Because the reader is made aware of the connection between I and H, when the signifier I appears in the text the temptation or impulse is there to read it as if it is the name of a character, as if it is a third- rather than a first-person pronoun. This destabilizes the very foundations of autobiography, a genre of writing which relies on the uniqueness of the writing I for its definition. The I is central to the project of autobiography (it is, after all, 'self-life-writing'). In one of the most influential studies of the genre, Philippe Lejeune wrote in his 1973 essay, 'The Autobiographical Pact', that autobiography can be defined as a 'narrative written by a real person concerning his [*sic*] own existence, where the focus is his individual life, in particular the story of his personality'.[25] In order for his definition to work, Lejeune says that the critic must be able to distinguish between autobiography proper and autobiographical fiction (in which a fictional narrator gives an account, in the first-person, of their 'individual life' and 'the story of [their] personality'). Therefore, Lejeune states, it is a necessary condition of autobiography that 'The *author*, the *narrator*, and the *protagonist* ... be identical' (p. 5). In contrast, Cixous's non-autobiographical 'I' remarks: ' "Author" is a pseudonym that should fool no one' (*Promethea*, p. 11).[26] It is conceded that neither H nor I could have written the book on their own – nor could the book have come into being without the contributions of Promethea (see p. 13). The voice and the subject of the narrative are constantly shifting. There is slippage and confusion between I and H (see pp. 16, 209), as well as between I and Promethea (see p. 139). The narrators and Promethea have an understanding of each other that extends beyond words (see p. 21). Interestingly, in terms of the connections between the body and the 'feminine' Imaginary previously discussed in Chapter 2, there is also an admission in *Promethea* that writing has its limits when it comes to representing Promethea, that there are aspects of Promethea that exceed or exist outside of language: 'All I can promise is to take down faithfully the words Promethea says out loud in French. As for all the rest, I make no guarantees' (p. 22).

In addition to dividing her narrative voice/self in *Promethea*, Cixous also takes a different approach to the style of her fiction. *Promethea* is significantly more conventional in form compared with the other fictions by Cixous written prior to and around the time of its composition. It may well be that the influence of Clarice Lispector is again at work. Although Lispector's writing does engage in forms of experimentation, these are usually so light of touch as to be almost invisible. As a result of this, the presence of the other in Lispector's texts is that much more accessible to the reader than would be the case in a text (such as Cixous's *Neutre*) whose stylistic experimentation, though well intended, unwittingly drowns out or obscures the voice of the other. One can see a shift towards a less cryptic style of writing taking place at the start of *Promethea* where it is explained that it will be I who will be writing the opening pages, rather than H: 'For a week H has struggled in vain . . . her efforts so far have produced nothing written other than convulsions, trancelike humming, and a hypnotizing/hypnotized state' (pp. 5–6). The narrators realize that the tools and methods they have been used to using up to this point are no longer suitable for the task. What had worked before when dealing with the abstract, no longer suffices when faced with 'reality in person in the specific person of Promethea' (p. 6). H therefore busies herself with 'burning old books, manuals, professional papers, theoretical volumes' (p. 6), clearing away the clutter of the past from the space of writing. I performs a similar operation with her body, reporting that she has 'ordered new hands, to caress you and to write you, hands that will fit you' (p. 42). These moves can be seen as suggestive of the fact that the stripping away of the self advocated at the end of *Angst* is beginning to be put into practice in *Promethea*. As well as making room for the other, this opens up the text to the reader (who can be thought of as another incarnation of the other). *Promethea* succeeds in drawing the reader into the narrative to a much greater degree than Cixous's earlier texts had done. Humour plays an important part in this process (*Promethea* is in fact a delightful, thoroughly entertaining book to read). Also significant are the many doubts, ideas and debates I, H and Promethea have over the writing of the book – all of which involve the reader as both an observer and a participant in the book's creation. The narrators (partially) release the text from their control, giving it a degree of extra-authorial freedom. Pondering a 'disorganized' notebook in which she has written of her day-to-day life with Promethea, I feels 'obliged' to present it to the reader 'in its authentic, immediate state' (p. 61). Likewise, on the penultimate page, Promethea expresses the wish that the narrators do not 'end' the book, as such, but instead hand over its reins to the reader to do with as they choose: 'It's all up to *you* now' (p. 210), Promethea informs the reader.

Promethea manages to 'give' itself to the reader – to a certain extent – and takes some significant steps towards the achievement of an *écriture féminine*. However, it can be argued that *Promethea* still falls short because the other it writes remains very personal (Promethea is an intimate, known other). For there to be an *écriture féminine*, in the widest possible understanding of the term, the writer must be able to bring the outside world, the truly 'other' into her writing. This dynamic between what might be characterized as the 'inner' and the 'outer' is illustrated by a frequently cited passage in *Vivre l'orange*. In this passage Cixous has been concentrating her whole being on the question of the orange for three days, 'seventy-two hours' (p. 20). Suddenly, the telephone rings and a voice enquires: "And Iran?" (p. 22). This interruption to her internal reverie, a reminder of an upcoming demonstration in support of the women of Iran, reconnects her with external events. She understands that a place must be found for the women of Iran, for the East, for history, in the 'inner Orient' of her writing (p. 20). In terms of Cixous's writing, this realization takes several years to bear fruit. *Promethea* is an important staging point along the way, but in order to achieve the full effect she desires – a writing where the political exists alongside and with the personal – Cixous finds that it is necessary to move some distance away from the world of fiction and embrace the world of the theatre instead.

The realm of characters

In her 'Conversations' with the members of the Centre d'Etudes Féminines Cixous explains why, in the mid-1980s, she moved her writing into the theatre: 'I found the only way I could deal with politics – poetically – was by changing genres' (p. 153). The need to maintain this connection with the poetic is important (see Chapters 4 and 6). Cixous's poetically political writing for the theatre in the mid-1980s has a tremendous impact on the continuing development of the idea of an *écriture féminine*. The flowering of Cixous's theatrical writing in this period, the understanding she reaches about the specific nature and otherness of the theatre, is the result of another remarkable and highly significant 'meeting'. Just as Clarice Lispector's work breathes new life into Cixous's approach to a 'feminine' form of writing, so too does Cixous's involvement with the director Ariane Mnouchkine and the company of actors at the Théâtre du Soleil reinvigorate and revitalize her entire writing project.

In the 1970s Cixous's writing for the theatre had been limited to two plays and one libretto: *La Pupille* (*The Pupil*),[27] *Portrait of Dora* and *The Name of Oedipus*. Although these works feature certain 'theatrical' effects not possible in fiction (such as, for instance, the sequences of still and moving film projected onto an on-stage screen during *Portrait of Dora*, or the parallel singing 'voices' in *Oedipus*), on the whole there is little to differentiate them, neither in form nor in content, from Cixous's fictional writing.[28] In the mid-1980s, however, Cixous's writing for the theatre becomes much more recognizably 'theatrical' – it also moves East. *La Prise de l'école de Madhubaï* (*The Conquest of the School at Madhubaï*), written soon after *Promethea*, is set in contemporary India and is based on the life-story of Phoolan Devi, the so-called 'Bandit Queen'.[29] Asia is also the setting for the first plays to emerge from Cixous's collaboration with Mnouchkine and the Théâtre du Soleil (a collaboration that is still ongoing): *L'Histoire terrible mais inachevée de Norodom Sihanouk, roi du Cambodge* (*The Terrible but Unfinished Story of Norodom Sihanouk, King of Cambodia*), first performed on 11 September 1985; and *L'Indiade, ou l'Inde de leurs rêves, et quelques écrits sur le théâtre* (*The Indiad, or the India of Their Dreams, and some writings on the theatre*), first performed on 30 September 1987.[30] The role of Mnouchkine and the actors of the Théâtre du Soleil in the writing of *Sihanouk* and *L'Indiade* is worth reflecting upon. The Théâtre du Soleil was founded in 1964 (its first production was an adaptation of *Les Petits Bourgeois* by Maxime Gorky). From its foundation, it has always operated as a collective entity. Mnouchkine and the actors work together, through improvization and experiment, to 'write' the plays they perform. In fact, the four plays performed by the company between 1969 and 1975 – *Les Clowns* (1969), *1789* (1970–71), *1793* (1972–73) and *L'Age d'or* (1975) – bear the words 'création collective' where one would usually find the name of an 'author'. One can therefore see that, in writing for the Théâtre du Soleil, Cixous found herself in the position of being asked to take a very different approach to her work.

Used to working in isolation, Cixous now found herself working alongside others, talking and listening to others – watching her writing take shape and transform itself in the hands and voices of others. In 'A Realm of Characters', an interview with Susan Sellers, Cixous describes some of the processes that she went through as *Sihanouk* and *L'Indiade* came to be written.[31] Cixous relates that she and Mnouchkine discussed 'a number of hypotheses' before settling on the themes of each play (p. 127). Mnouchkine appears to have contributed significantly to the chosen themes. Like *The Conquest of the School at Madhubaï* (which Cixous wrote 'independently', so to speak), *Sihanouk* and *L'Indiade* explore the impact of 'history' on the life of the individual. This was also the theme explored in the early 1980s by the Théâtre du Soleil when they performed two of Shakespeare's 'history' plays (as well as one of his comedies).[32] The influence of Shakespeare (and by implication the Théâtre du Soleil) is writ large all over *Sihanouk* and *L'Indiade*. Although Cixous had previously used examples and quotations from Shakespeare in her writing,[33] what makes *Sihanouk* and *L'Indiade* different is that Cixous now adopts recognizably 'Shakespearean' structures and forms. Both *Sihanouk* and *L'Indiade* follow the example of Shakespeare in seeing history through the eyes of the 'high' and the 'low'.[34] The layout of the dialogue on the page and the manner in which the characters deliver this dialogue are strongly reminiscent of Shakespeare (again, like the Joycean touches in her writing, the impression given of a certain 'Shakespeareanism' is felt on an instinctual rather than a wholly verbal level).[35] Like Shakespeare's plays, both *Sihanouk* and *L'Indiade* are written in five acts (like *Henry IV*, *Sihanouk* is in two parts – one of many points of comparison between these two plays). In addition to these touches of Shakespeare, other changes have taken place. The timelines of *Sihanouk* and *L'Indiade* are on a grander, more 'epic' scale than Cixous's earlier theatrical writing. Unlike the span of a single day in which the story of *The Conquest of the School at Madhubaï* unfolds,[36] the action in *Sihanouk* and *L'Indiade* takes place over a period of many years. *Sihanouk* progresses from the king's abdication in 1955 (so he can take up a role in politics as prime minister) to the rise to power two decades later of Pol Pot's Khmer Rouge in 1975. *L'Indiade* has as its background the final decade of the struggle for

Indian independence and the events leading up to the violence surrounding the division of the sub-continent and the creation of Pakistan in 1947.[37] *Sihanouk* and *L'Indiade* also have a considerably larger cast of characters (and thus, by implication require a much larger cast of actors) than Cixous's earlier plays – as well as a much wider range of locations. All of these various new theatrical elements that are found in *Sihanouk* and *L'Indiade* are made possible when one is working with a company, such as the Théâtre du Soleil, that is used to putting on large-scale, complex theatrical projects. Although there are other, more personal reasons why Cixous undertakes such vast theatrical projects, the influence of the Théâtre du Soleil cannot be ignored.

As she explains in 'A Realm of Characters', once she and Mnouchkine had reached agreement on the theme of each play, Cixous would set off on 'months of painstaking historical research' before settling down to write (p. 127). However, even when Cixous had 'written' a play, changes would still take place. Cixous found that the process of putting on a theatrical production, particularly in the case of a company such as the Théâtre du Soleil (who spend a considerable period of time in rehearsal), helps to keep a play from settling into a final and conclusive text:

> During rehearsals thousands of things happen which bring about changes in the play. Not in the text, the text stays the same. But in the overall timing and construction of the play. For instance, no writer can say in advance how long a scene will take. A scene may be played more or less slowly, and scene-changes can dictate as much as twenty minutes of extra space. So when I write, I write with plenty of breath. I write without worrying about the time, concentrating on the heart of each scene, on giving the characters everything they need in order to live. Then, as rehearsals get under way, I cut. So there are always several versions of the play.
>
> (pp. 127–8)

The accounts Cixous gives of her collaboration with Mnouchkine and the Théâtre du Soleil have strong affinities with the descriptions she gives elsewhere of *écriture féminine*. Cixous's writing for the Théâtre du Soleil can be construed as a freely given gift, a writing that is open to the other, a writing that does not settle on a single, 'phallocentric' meaning/text. Cixous's thoughts and reflections on what this collaboration has meant to both her writing and her views on writing are discussed at length in 'From the Scene of the Unconscious ...' and in the 'écrits sur le théâtre' ('writings on the theatre') that are included in the back of the Théâtre du Soleil edition of *L'Indiade* (pp. 247–78).

In 'From the Scene of the Unconscious ...' Cixous explains the attraction of writing for the theatre. It is, she considers, 'the most marvellous place for someone who writes' (p. 12). Cixous describes the theatre as 'the *immediate* site of the desire of the other' (p. 12; see also Chapter 6). She considers that the theatre is the space in which the writer and her writing are in the closest possible contact with the other, in all its forms. The immediacy of the theatre, in terms of time, creates writing that operates through a kind of 'violent condensation' (p. 16). Cixous argues that writing for the theatre cannot indulge in long passages of reflection or diversion – pausing for an unspecified length of time here, wandering off in unknown directions there. On the contrary, she explains: 'One must lose neither time nor attention. No detours ... The look of the spectator should go straight to the actor's heart' (p. 16). Cixous considers that the theatre is also an immediate physical space – a space in which one is brought into close proximity and made aware of the existence of many others. In the theatre, one needs to accommodate or account for the presence of an audience, as well as both the actors and the characters on the stage.[38] This is achieved, from the author's point of view, through the kind of 'letting go' Cixous talks about in 'Sorties' and *Angst*. The author of a play finds herself placed in a very similar role to that of an actor in a play – both, Cixous says, have need of a sense of 'self that has almost evaporated' (p. 9). Just as an 'actor is someone whose ego is reserved and humble enough for the other to be able to invade and occupy him', so must an author 'reach this state of "*démoïsation*", this state of without me, of depossession of the self, that will make possible the *possession* of the author by the characters' (p. 13). The question of characters is central to Cixous's theatrical writing. As Cixous remarks in 'A Realm of Characters': 'Writing for the theatre, I am haunted by a universe of fictitious but real people ... I live, inhabited by my characters' (p. 126). Because of this, in the theatre the boundaries between writer and text are broken down, they become fluid. The writer is no longer just writing her own body, she is writing the bodies of all those who 'inhabit' her. Or, rather, it is 'they' who are doing the writing. In 'Qui es-tu?' ('Who are you?'), one of the 'écrits sur le théâtre' in *L'Indiade*, Cixous describes the part played by her characters in the writing of a play:

> J'ouvre la porte. Ils entrent . . . Il règne sur le plateau une liberté qui ne dépend plus d'aucun auteur, mais seulement de leurs destins à eux [I open the door. They enter . . . On the stage there reigns a freedom that no longer depends on any author, but only on their own destinies.   (p. 276)

One consequence of this is that because she is writing through the body of the character (or actor) it becomes possible for Cixous to 'write' the *jouissance* of a man. As she notes in 'From the Scene of the Unconscious . . .', as 'a woman' who writes 'with the body' she had 'never dared create a male character in fiction', reasoning that a man's *jouissance* was always destined to remain unknown to her (p. 15).[39] However, in the theatre no such rules or restrictions apply:

> No, our creatures lack nothing, not penises, not breasts, not kidneys, not bellies . . . This is the present that theatre makes to the author: incarnation. It permits the male author to create women who will not be feigned, and the woman author is granted the chance to create perfectly constituted men!   (p. 15)

In terms of *écriture féminine*, the theatre has much to offer. In writing for the theatre, through the interaction that takes place between the writer and the character/actor, or the play and audience, Cixous finds that it is possible for the other to 'inhabit' and be involved in her writing to a previously unprecedented degree. Not only can Cixous write real flesh and blood characters, but she can create fully 'incarnated' male characters. It becomes possible for her to 'know', if only at second hand, the *jouissance* of a man. However, in terms of *écriture féminine*, the theatre also has its drawbacks. For instance, in addition to altering the writer's relationship with her characters, the nature of the theatre means that the timeline or chronology of a play is often very different from that of a work of fiction. As Cixous observes in 'Qui es-tu?', in the theatre 'la vérité du personnage est dans l'instant: immédiate, précise, éphémère et poignante [the truth of the character is in the moment: immediate, precise, ephemeral and poignant]' (p. 275). This difference can be seen in the kind of writing Cixous produces in each genre. Whereas, as she notes in 'A Realm of Characters', with her fiction she can allow the 'meaning' of her writing to 'gather slowly' – giving the reader of her text 'the whole of eternity if she wishes', in the theatre time is limited, finite: 'there must be an immediate explosion of meaning ... Theatre is the art of urgency. Everything happens in the present' (p. 126). Though this urgency can be seen as a positive aspect of her writing, particularly in terms of Cixous's idea of 'writing in the present' (see Chapter 4), it can also serve to inhibit the kind of lingering, prolonged act of loving and living with the other that is explored in texts such as *Vivre l'orange* and *Promethea*. It limits the poetic excess or 'waste' Cixous feels *écriture féminine* ought to produce. With its perceived emphasis on the 'message', the theatre (or at least the kind of theatrical writing Cixous is engaged in up to this point – see below) does not allow for the same degree of reflection and meditation on the 'medium' that is such a feature of Cixous's fiction. *Sihanouk* and *L'Indiade* do not explore the processes of writing in the manner in which, for example, I, H and Promethea discuss how they are going to write *Promethea*.[40] In this respect, *Sihanouk* and *L'Indiade* fall short of the kind of self-aware, or self-reflective writing Cixous appears to be advocating in her descriptions of *écriture féminine*. Despite her evident enthusiasm for the theatre, in the texts immediately following *L'Indiade* Cixous returns to the genre of fiction, bringing with her the lessons she has learned from her theatrical writing.

In defence of (poetic) writing

Manne aux Mandelstams aux Mandelas (*Manna for the Mandelstams for the Mandelas*), Cixous's first fiction after *L'Indiade*, carries on with many of the themes that she had been exploring in her writing for the Théâtre du Soleil.[41] Like *Promethea*, *Manna* is a book of love. It is also a book of exile and separation, a book that examines the ways in which love can be sustained in the face of terrible events. *Manna* opens up windows into the inner lives of individuals caught up in the cycle of violence and oppression that runs through much of twentieth-century 'history'.[42] Because it was composed in such close proximity to *Sihanouk* and *L'Indiade* it is tempting to read the fragmentary nature of the fiction, its division into named chapters, subheadings and interludes, its use of parallel narratives (running from the Mandelas in South Africa, to the Mandelstams in the Soviet Union, to the narrator/author in France), as if they might be comparable to the manner in which a play is divided into a number of acts and scenes. *Manna* certainly displays a variety of theatrical touches. Cixous's description in the opening pages of the text of the connection she senses between herself and Winnie Mandela (also referred to as Zami) strongly evokes the account she gives in 'From the Scene of the Unconscious ...' of how the author of a play is 'possessed' by her characters: 'Her feet pace a soil at the bottom of my breast. If it sees the light of day, this book will be the fruit of a haunting ... she has won me over, invaded and overwhelmed me' (p. 9). Likewise, Cixous draws on her experience of writing for the theatre in order to introduce, for the first time, 'complete' male characters into her fiction (i.e. Nelson Mandela and Osip Mandelstam). However, *Manna* also differs from her theatrical writing – particularly in its self-examination, its running commentary on the medium of writing. The narrator of the fiction, the 'I', appears frequently in *Manna*, both to comment on the manner in which the text is progressing and on her own thoughts and limitations: 'This book is an attempt at compassion. Only an attempt, for I am capable of going to the foot of the olive trees, but I will never manage to feel in my feet the nails Sergeant Visser drove into the feet of old Willie Smit, in spite of the supplication and tears' (p. 15; see also, for example, p. 138). Such 'metafictional' interactions introduce an ambiguity, lacking in the theatre, which makes it far from easy to distinguish between the voice of the writer and the voice(s) of the subject(s) of her writing. The 'I' of the narrator is often slipping in and out of the 'I' of the characters. For instance, whose 'supplication and tears' does the previous quotation refer to? Are they Willie Smit's, or the author's? It all depends how one reads it, where the emphasis falls. Likewise, in the following passage from 12 June 1960, when Nelson Mandela has just been released from prison and the reader is informed that he will return there in four years' time (when he is condemned to a life sentence), it is open to question as to whether it is the voice of Winnie Mandela or the author who is speaking in the first-person:

> This is how I live, letter by letter, holding back the present by all its hands, by each one of its fingers as though I knew what I do not know, it is fear that is my law. Prudently, deliciously, Zami lives in a delicate avarice. She, she has all the time.   (p. 136)

The transformative (and dangerous) power of language and writing – a key concern of *écriture féminine* – is ever-present in the background of *Manna*. Osip Mandelstam's fate is sealed in 1933 when he writes a thinly veiled satire on Stalin: 'sixteen heavy-footed lines ... a dance of death around the broad-chested Osset' (p. 140).[43] The two strands of the narrative close the text with the themes of missing words and precious, life-preserving pieces of writing: the 'prison' letters between Winnie and Nelson Mandela (see pp. 227–41); and Osip Mandelstam's 'posthumous poem', 'Lines about the Unknown Soldier'[44] – one of the poems which Akhmatova and Nadezhda Mandelstam recite to each other to keep memory and hope alive (see pp. 253–4). Writing is depicted in *Manna* as something that is under threat, fragile and transient – yet, at the same time, enduring (in both senses of the word).

Although the subject of writing has always been an important aspect of Cixous's work, it is significant that in the fictional texts that follow *Manna* – firstly *Jours de l'an* (*FirstDays of the Year*),[45] and then *L'Ange au secret* (*The Angel in Secret*) and *Déluge* (*Deluge*)[46] – writing emerges into the foreground to become the principal focus of poetic exploration and thought. In an interview conducted around the time of *Manna*, Cixous suggests a possible reason for this change in emphasis: 'The language of the mass media ... has fallen on us like a curse in the last generation ... writing at this point means more than it did when I began.'[47] Just as Cixous's original vision of *écriture féminine* in the 1970s had been conceived as a means of setting up 'lines of defence' around the concept of the 'feminine', in the age of the mass media it is writing, *écriture*, which she considers to be the thing most immediately under attack.

As Cixous explains: 'The mass media not only produce a discourse that has completely excluded everything that can be poetic language but furthermore combat poetic language as dangerous, demented, or obviously useless' (p. 33). One might say that the mass media have become, in Cixous's view, the new harbingers of 'phallocentric' discourse: the purveyors of a 'glorious phallic monosexuality' (*The Newly Born Woman*, p. 85), the destroyers of difference. Cixous's commitment to the cause of poetic writing is clearly signalled in the opening words of *FirstDays*. Strongly evoking Cixous's descriptions of *écriture féminine*, this text begins: 'Writing has returned, the stream, the slender silent stream with its singing arms . . . silent words flowing from one community to the other, from one life to the other' (p. 3).[48] Cixous is at pains in *First-Days* to differentiate between herself, 'Hélène Cixous', and the 'author' of the fiction. It is noticeable that the manner in which she does this is very different from the method she had employed in *Promethea* (where she splits her narrative voice into I and H). The experience of writing for the theatre can once again be seen to be playing a role in creating this difference. As was the case in *Manna* (where the voice of the narrative is 'possessed' or taken over by the characters), the 'author' of *FirstDays* emerges from within the state of '*démoïsation*' Cixous had discovered in her writing for the theatre: 'Why do I speak of the author as if she were not me? Because she isn't me. She departs from me and goes where I don't want to go . . . Ungovernable. Freed' (p. 101). After the exploration of the other in history that her writing engages in during the mid- to late 1980s, with *FirstDays* Cixous returns to an exploration of the 'personal'. However, *FirstDays* is engaged in a form of 'personal' writing that is very different from the introspective exploration of the 'I' found in Cixous's early fiction. This again can be traced to the effect of the state of '*démoïsation*' Cixous mentions in 'From the Scene of the Unconscious . . .': its trajectory in this case comparable with the move Clarice Lispector takes in her final text, *The Hour of the Star*, to 'inhabit' the body and soul of a man in order to achieve the proper distance from which to narrate the life story of the street-girl Macabea.[49] As Cixous writes in 'The Author in Truth', Lispector's depossession of her self opens the way for the other in a spectacular and unprecedented manner:

> It can happen that an author, a woman, comes too close to a woman to get to make her acquaintance, in the sense of discovering her still unknown. And thus, through familiarity, she misses her. What to do? A trip around the world to make an entrance from the other side, this time as a stranger.   (p. 175)

Cixous's insistence that the 'author' of *FirstDays* 'isn't me' can therefore be thought of as the result of an equivalent journey away from and a consequent return to the (newly 'strange') scene of writing. However, unlike Lispector's narrator, the 'author' of *FirstDays* does not 'arrive' back from this journey – at least, not completely. The point of arrival is held in perpetual abeyance. The 'author' expresses her fear of 'discovering the truth' (p. 11), of reaching the final point of (no) return. She explains this fear in terms of an analogy with the work of the Japanese printmaker Katsushika Hokusai (1760–1849), who, Cixous's 'author' relates, spent 'his entire life' producing coloured woodcuts of Mount Fujiyama (p. 11). The reason Hokusai could continue to do this, she contends, was his knowledge of 'the impossibility of ever painting Fujiyama' (p. 11). It was this, she argues, that 'authorized' him to carry on: 'For if it ever came to pass that one succeeded in painting what one had dreamed of painting since the very first paintbrush, everything would perish on the spot ... A stony completion would seize the universe' (p. 11).

This trope of 'returning' to the same theme, exploring the same subjects from different angles, has always been a feature of Cixous's work (consider the 'dix livres/ten books' on the subject of 'la mort/ death' that led up to *Angst*). This cycle of return and renewal is an important manifestation of Cixous's vision of the 'poetic' (see Chapter 4 for a full discussion on this point). Although there is a greater diversity in terms of themes and settings, both temporally and geographically, in Cixous's recent (post *L'Indiade*) texts, many of the preoccupations of her earlier writing are still much in evidence. *Déluge* returns to some of the sensations of pain and abandonment that ran through *Angst*. *L'Ange au secret*, like many of her fictions, past and present, is a richly 'intertextual' work.[50] The composition of Cixous's 1997 fiction, *Or, les lettres de mon père* (*Gold, My Father's Letters*), is sparked by the chance discovery of her father's long-lost correspondence (returning her, albeit very differently – as a 'stranger' – to her first work of fiction, *Inside*).[51] Her 1993 fiction, *Beethoven à jamais ou l'existence de Dieu* (*Immortal Beethoven or the Existence of God*), explores the issues of sexual difference, the relations between the self and the other, and the themes of death and god – all of which are central to many of her early texts.[52] Interestingly, *Beethoven à jamais* also reworks the interactions explored in *Manna* between the 'historical' Mandelstams and the 'contemporary' Mandelas, doing so with reference to an unnamed contemporary couple and to the relationship between the composer Beethoven and his anonymous 'Immortal Beloved' (to whom he writes a famously mysterious letter). The fate of the individual (the other) in history continues to be a major subject of exploration and experiment. Cixous's 1992 translation of Aeschylus's *The Furies* (for a production by the Théâtre du Soleil) leads directly into the composition of her 1994 play (for the same company): *La Ville parjure ou le réveil des Erinyes* (*The Perjured City or the Awakening of the Furies*).[53] Another 'historical' theatrical text, also from 1994, *L'Histoire* (*qu'on ne connaîtra jamais*) [*The Story/History* (*which we will never know*)], travels back to medieval Iceland to recount the story/history of the thirteenth-century poet Snorri Sturlusson.[54] The Norse gods transport Sturlusson back in time into the distant, mythical past, so he can witness the actual events described in the *Niebelungenlied* saga. This course of events allows Cixous to use *L'Histoire* to engage in a detailed on-stage exploration of the medium of the theatre. Although her fiction has always had an element of the genre of metafiction about it, the metatheatricality of *L'Histoire* is an aspect of her theatrical writing that had been previously underdeveloped. Cixous's 1999 play, *Tambours sur la digue: sous forme de pièce ancienne pour marionnettes jouée par des acteurs* (*Drums on the Embankment: In the Form of an Ancient Play for Marionettes Played by Actors*), follows a similar metatheatrical path: drawing on the traditions of Japanese bunraku puppet theatre (as well as the versatility and physical virtuosity of the company at the Théâtre du Soleil) to explore the role of the actor as a 'performer' in the creation of the meaning of a theatrical text.[55]

The engagement with 'history' in the fictional text *Manna*, together with the exploration of 'writing' in the theatrical texts,

L'Histoire and *Tambours sur la digue*, indicate that Cixous is able to freely cross over from fiction to theatre, theatre to fiction, letting each speak to and enhance the other. This interplay between her fiction and theatre is also evident in the third play Cixous publishes in 1994: *Voile Noire Voile Blanche/Black Sail White Sail* (published, like *Vivre l'orange*, as a bilingual text).[56] *Black Sail White Sail* continues where *Manna* left off – with Nadezhda Mandelstam, Anna Akhmatova and Akhmatova's friend, Lydia Chukovskaya, still struggling to keep writing alive in the years immediately after the death of Stalin.[57] Uncertainty looms large in this text. The poet Boris Pasternak is listed as 'The Present-Absences', three others, Osip Mandelstam, Akhmatova's first husband, Nikolai Gumilev (who was executed in 1921) and their son, Lev Gumilev (arrested and deported in 1937 and 1949), are given as 'The Absent-Presences' (p. 223). These characters 'interact' with those on the stage. Osip Mandelstam 'haunts' every scene. Akhmatova is kept waiting for news of her imprisoned son (who may or may not be alive), as well as an edition of her poems (which may or may not be published). Cixous as playwright hands the reins of the text over to those who are recreating it in the theatre. Noting that the three main characters, Akhmatova, Nadezhda Mandelstam and Chukovskaya, 'address each other using countless little Russian nicknames', Cixous gives the direction: 'The actresses will use these whenever they feel the need' (p. 223). Like *Promethea*, *Black Sail White Sail* concludes with its gaze turned outward, towards the reader/audience (p. 351):

Akhmatova
(*To the audience*) You who live later, have you heard of Osip and of his wife here present? And of Anna Akhmatova?

   I'd so like to know. One would have to die, to skip a century, and return.

Nadezhda
Or receive a telegram from the future: Poems arrived safely. Signed: the shore of the 21st century.

Lydia
Anna Akhmatova: Complete Works.

In addition to being a play about the conflict between 'history' and writing, *Black Sail White Sail* is also a play about the daily lives of elderly women. In this respect, one can connect it with Cixous's current writing about her mother.

With *Osnabrück* (1999) Cixous begins to write in earnest about her mother – motivated by what she identifies in 'From the Scene of the Unconscious ...' as the sense that a writer 'must not forget' that 'Writing is (should be) the act of reminding oneself of what is ... remembering what could disappear' (p. 7).[58] As Cixous explains in the interview printed in this current book (see Chapter 6), the realization that her mother, who is now in her nineties, will die, prompted her to begin writing what would otherwise disappear entirely. *Osnabrück* chronicles and preserves a whole series of family stories from the time before Cixous's birth (Cixous's mother is originally from Osnabrück). Cixous continues this important personal project in the two texts she publishes in 2000: *Le jour où je n'étais pas là* (*The Day I Wasn't There*) and *Les Rêveries de la femme sauvage* (*Reveries of the Wild Woman*).[59] In these two texts, Cixous relates a number of stories from her own childhood, many of her mother's memories of working at her clinic in post-war Algiers, and the minutiae of Cixous's relationship with her mother, past and present. The narrative of *Le jour* picks up on and reworks many of the strands discussed above. There are, for instance, stories of giving birth and of Cixous's mother's clinic, the birth of one of Cixous's own sons (and the issues this raises of otherness, disadvantage and disability), an exploration of the interplay between Cixous's feelings of exile *in* Algeria, and her feelings of exile *from* Algeria, reflections on her Jewishness and the fate of the Jews, guilt, death (the baby's, the grandmother's), abandonment (of the baby, of the three-legged dog she comes across in the woods, and of the Romanian orphan, Irena) and writing. As was the case with *Promethea*, the obligations placed on a writer when she is in close proximity to her subject is one of the central concerns of *Le jour*. In *Le jour*, Cixous not only struggles with the writing of the book itself, but with the ethics of writing down her own mother's 'secrets':

> Pourquoi autrement me confierait-elle soigneusement tous les secrets avec la notice ⟨⟨à ne pas publier⟩⟩ si ce n'est pour attirer mon

attention sur ses trésors les plus cachés et les plus dangereux . . . Elle
me dit ne le répète pas. J'entends bien l'inflexion. Cela veut dire
fais-le et ne me le dis pas . . . Tout ce que je te raconte c'est pour trahir.
J'ai confié. Maintenant prends ta lance et brandis-la. *Deine Lanze*
c'est ainsi qu'elle appelle mon stylo [Why otherwise would she
confide to me with such care all the secrets with the warning "do not
publish" unless to draw my attention to her most hidden her most
perilous treasures . . . She tells me don't repeat it. I catch the
inflection. That means do it and don't tell me . . . Everything I am
telling you it's to betray. I have confided. Now take up your sword
and brandish it. *Deine Lanze* that is what she calls my pen].   (p. 145)

Although it deals with many serious issues, *Le jour* is also a delight-
fully funny book. Cixous uses humour to great effect to convey the
individualism and unique characteristics of her mother (see, for
instance, the description on p. 100 of her difficulties in talking with
her mother, now that 'elle ne quitte jamais sa petite radio portative
[she is never without her little portable radio]').

Le jour is also a book about animals. The story of her 'chien à trois
pattes [three-legged dog]' (p. 17) is just one of many instances
in which animals have come to figure strongly in Cixous's recent
writing. There are, for instance, stories of her relationship with
(and abandonment of) dogs in 'Stigmata, or Job the dog' and *Les
Rêveries*, as well as tales of cats in *Messie* and 'Shared at dawn'.[60]
In *Le jour* Cixous also considers the fate of battery chickens (see
pp. 102–6), highlighting, as she explains in the interview printed
in this present book: 'The ignominious way animals are treated . . .
it's just a form of holocaust . . . for me there is no separation, no *strict*
separation between animals and human beings' (see Chapter 6).
Cixous's relationship with animals adds yet another dimension to
her thinking on the nature of the other and otherness. On the one
hand, as she explains in another interview, Cixous sees this relationship in metaphorical, dream-like terms: 'animals are important
for me because I can't imagine human beings other than as animals
in transition . . . I need the instinctiveness and the wildness in a
human being. So, when I meet people in reality, or in dreams,
there's always a kind of animal awake in the person.'[61] On the
other hand, as is seen in the interview in Chapter 6, as well as in
her short story 'Shared at dawn', Cixous is keen to explore the

possibility of a genuine 'moment of communion' between humans and animals (*Stigmata*, p. 178). 'Shared at dawn' is about the discovery of a seemingly dead bird and of the desire of her cat, Thea, for the body and life of this bird. Although she 'recognize[s] the rights animals have among themselves' (p. 178), as a human Cixous still instinctually intervenes when the dead bird suddenly comes to life in her hands. Not wanting 'something to die in my house' (p. 178), she catches the bird and releases it out of the window. However, in doing this, she is faced with the anguish and 'sorrow' of Thea (p. 179), who searches in vain all day for the now missing bird. Cixous realizes that, in acting as a human, she has 'betrayed' her cat (p. 179). This realization leads her into the position of imagining herself in Thea's place, behaving as Thea would do, becoming genuinely other: 'oh my god if that bird comes back I will give it to her, I swear . . . yes, if it came back, I too would play with its lukewarm little body, I'd give it sharp little blows with my paw and I'd slit its throat cheerfully' (p. 179).

The rich variety and achievement of Cixous's recent writing might be taken as an indication that the aims of the project of *écriture féminine* have at last been attained. Certainly, Cixous's more recent fiction and theatrical writing is much more open to and connected with the other. It comfortably crosses from genre to genre, past to present, 'inside' to 'outside' (even human to animal). It also avoids the impulse to 'close' on a singular 'phallocentric' meaning and, as was the case with *Promethea*, it manages to do this with much less of the formal experimentation and word-play that was found to be (potentially) problematic in her earlier writing. Yet, this assumption about *écriture féminine* is also fraught with difficulties. The uncertainties in many of these texts, the 'fear' of 'a stony completion' that haunts the 'author' of *FirstDays*, for instance, suggest that there is still a sense that Cixous's writing is seeking for, reaching towards an undefinable 'something' – answers to questions that she has not yet fully understood. To a much greater extent than was the case in her early texts, Cixous's recent writing is concerned with what she refers to in her 'Conversations' with the members of the Centre d'Etudes Féminines as 'the struggle to think politically via a poetic route' (p. 152). Poetic writing has always been present in Cixous's vision of *écriture féminine*, but over the years, partly through the emergence of the mass media, partly through Cixous's involvement with the Théâtre du Soleil, partly through the changes brought about by the natural growth and development of her writing, the idea of the 'poetic' – in both writing *and* thought – has taken on a whole new level of importance and urgency.

Chapter 4

Poetic theory

What is most true is poetic.   (*Rootprints*, p. 3)

In his introductory words to one of the Wellek Library Lectures in Critical Theory given by Cixous at the University of California, Irvine, in May 1990 – a series of lectures that have been translated and published as *Three Steps on the Ladder of Writing* – Jacques Derrida comments that Cixous's achievement as a writer rests on the fact that she is 'a poet-thinker, very much a poet and a very thinking poet'.[1] The implication behind Derrida's words is that the kind of 'poetic' writing Cixous is involved in comes about through a system of underlying thought processes that are altogether different from the concerns of standard ('masculine') philosophical discourse. Indeed, it has often been remarked (particularly by Cixous herself) that Cixous's poetic writing has much more in common with the art of painting than it does with the discipline of philosophy. Many of the examples Cixous uses in her more recent discussions of *écriture féminine* are drawn from the economy of painting. As she remarks in one of these essays, 'The Last Painting or the Portrait of God', in both writing and painting one is first and foremost concerned not with facts or certainties, but with 'mysteries' and 'questions'.[2] Just as Cixous's Hokusai knows that he will never be able to capture the true essence of Mount Fujiyama (see *FirstDays*, p. 11), Cixous's poetic writer knows that she will never fully understand or solve the problem which she has set her mind upon. The deferral of the moment of closure is crucial, both to Hokusai the painter, and to Cixous the poetic writer. It is in this refusal to reach a conclusion, in this willingness to admit that she may not complete her 'task' or 'quest', that Cixous's poetic writing can most clearly be differentiated from the concerns of standard philosophical discourse. As Cixous explains in one of her seminars at the Centre de Recherches en Etudes Féminines, it is once again a question of how one relates to and writes (about) the other: 'Philosophy has always wanted to think its other, to interiorize, incorporate it. From the moment it thinks its other, the other is no longer other but becomes the same. It enters into the space of what can be thought, it loses its strangeness' (*Readings*, p. 90). Cixous argues that although standard 'philosophical discourse ... can be developed rapidly in an abstract way', what it cannot accommodate or make room for is the unpredictability and freedom of that which is 'living' (p. 92). That which is alive, mobile, elusive, transient, mutable cannot be incorporated into (trapped by) standard philosophical discourse. In standard philosophy, the impulse is to gather the subject of thought 'in a noun', 'to capture' and 'plant' it so that it will put down roots and cling onto and draw its sustenance from whatever meaning or label has been ascribed to it (p. 112). Consequently, Cixous contends, standard philosophy has to content itself with the consideration of 'immobile objects' (p. 92). The practice of working on what moves, she argues, the practice of working 'on what escapes', is something that 'can only be done poetically' (p. 92).

(Poetic) writing is not arriving

What does it mean to work on a problem 'poetically'? For a start, it means making room for a certain degree of freedom in the sphere of interpretation. In poetry one is always attuned to or aware of the potential in words and phrases to mean more than they might at first appear to mean. Poetry is the art of attempting to convey the hidden, the unspoken, it draws upon the extra resources that lurk in the outer fringes of language (such as the non-space of the 'feminine' Imaginary). One can see this process taking place in Cixous's texts. For instance, in the last pages of *Promethea*, I, H and Promethea discuss what 'name' they shall give to their book – a discussion which takes the form of a game of 'What-If-We-Called-It' (p. 210). Following various serious and not so serious suggestions,

Promethea comes up with 'Promethea Falls in Love' (p. 211). At this point, the text ends with two lines of unattributed dialogue (p. 211):

— Falls?
— Is.

These lines can be read as a suggestion that the title should be 'Promethea Is in Love'. However, they can also be said to be an indication that Promethea simply 'is'. That is to say, in the final analysis the bald fact of her existence (her '*is*-ness') is all that can be gleaned from the pages of Promethea's book. From one point of view, therefore, the pages of her book appear to have been condensed and focused into one deceptively mundane, single, mysterious word. However, as Cixous points out in the interview in this present book, appearances can be deceptive. The French word '*est*' ('is') can also be translated as 'east', as Cixous remarks: 'that's how the language plays: in several directions and at several levels' (see Chapter 6). Any attempts to close off or finish the book are thwarted by the 'poetic' resources of language. Looked at from this alternate, poetic point of view, the book 'escapes' from its author(s). As Cixous notes in her essay 'Writing blind: Conversation with the donkey' (one of the essays collected in *Stigmata: Escaping Texts*), this potential for an excess of signification, present in even the most quotidian of words, means that as a writer she finds that she 'must play language quick and true like an honest musician, not leap over a single word-beat'.[3] The picture Cixous paints in this essay of the meticulous way in which she approaches her writing is extremely interesting, and illuminating. Cixous uses similar imagery in her 'Inter Views' with Mireille Calle-Gruber, where she explains that her writing does not emerge from an attempt at 'mastery', but rather it is the result of 'an exercise of virtuosity' (*Rootprints*, p. 38). The distinction between mastery and virtuosity lies in a subtle but highly significant shift of emphasis. Mastery suggests some degree of dominance over something or somebody else – it calls to mind the actions of the ('masculine') hierarchical system of 'Logocentrism' Cixous describes in 'Sorties' (see Chapter 2). Virtuosity, on the other hand, can be seen as indicative of a certain respectful ('feminine') process of interaction between the artist and his or her chosen medium. Just as some musicians can 'exercise virtuosity' through a process of concentration so intense that the instrument they are playing becomes something akin to an extension of their own body, Cixous's virtuosic writing forms complex, multidirectional pathways between language and the body, writing and the writer.

Another way in which Cixous's writing can be considered to work 'poetically' is the way in which the development, shape and direction taken by Cixous's fiction and theatrical writing (see Chapter 3) reflects the patterns found in the economy of a sequence of poems. Like a poet composing a sequence of poems, Cixous returns to and explores the same themes, topics and problems from a number of different perspectives. Cixous's oeuvre, her sequence of texts, does not offer up conclusive answers but, rather, takes the reader on a journey through her moods, frustrations, delights, discoveries and insights (as she admires and describes the instances of beauty, inspiration and revelation that occur along the way). Compare this with what happens in a sequence of poems such as, to use an example from a poet much admired by Cixous, Shakespeare's *Sonnets*.[4] In his *Sonnets* Shakespeare devotes 126 sonnets to an inconclusive exploration of the question of how the beauty of an anonymous young man (the 'lovely boy' of sonnet 126) is to be preserved; Shakespeare then writes a further 26 sonnets trying (and, arguably, failing) to make sense of the complex and seemingly destructive relationship between the poet (who might or might not be Shakespeare) and a mysterious (also anonymous) 'dark lady'. Again, no conclusion is reached. Even today, after centuries of scholarship, speculation and commentary have been devoted to its mysteries, Shakespeare's *Sonnets* still manages to ask more questions than it answers. Like one of Cixous's texts, each one of Shakespeare's sonnets can be read as a work of art in its own right. However, again like one of Cixous's texts, each sonnet is also part of a greater whole. No single Shakespearean sonnet, or Cixousian text, can hope to fully comprehend or express the mystery or question with which it is concerned. Instead, each sonnet, or text, is a meditation upon, a sketch of, or a brief insight into some small aspect of a wider, unknown (and possibly unknowable) strangeness.

In *Three Steps* Cixous comments that her writing often reaches towards the place 'where knowing and unknowing touch' (p. 38). The movement of her writing is two-fold: it works both towards 'the incomprehensible' – that which will always be unknown; and also towards 'the invisible' – that which is unknown, at present (p. 38). Just as Cixous's Hokusai is faced with painting the impossible (the unpaintable), Cixous embarks on the path to poetic writing by 'trying to think the unthinkable' (p. 38). The fact that the thing which she is setting out to do is in all probability unachievable is the very essence of its appeal. As Cixous remarks further on in *Three Steps*, what matters is not the direction in which one is heading, but the build up of momentum: 'One has to get going. This is what writing is, starting off ... This does not mean one will get there. Writing is not arriving; most of the time it's *not arriving*' (p. 65). Arguably, one can see Cixous's writing '*not arriving*' in the attempts she makes to create a writing of the other in her fiction and theatre. The fact that (like the Shakespeare of the *Sonnets*) it is open to question as to whether or not she actually ever achieves her goal should not be taken to mean that she has in any way failed in her writing. On the contrary, it is the journey, not the specific point of arrival that matters. In Cixous's case, however, it is also on occasion necessary to set off in the 'wrong' direction – that is, if one wishes to surprise oneself with new and unhoped for discoveries. As Cixous observes in *Three Steps*: 'writing is writing what you cannot know before you have written' (p. 38). These things that are not yet known are the 'mysteries' she speaks of in 'The Last Painting or the Portrait of God'. In order to make room for them, rather than approach her writing with a linear, closed-off mind (a mind that is doomed to repeat the mistakes of the past), Cixous adopts a strategy in which she is open and responsive to the unexpected. It is an approach to writing that relies on her being able to maintain an acute state of awareness, constantly ready to interrupt herself, prepared to head off in new directions when and however the mood or inspiration takes her. The way in which she does this, Cixous remarks in 'Writing blind', is to 'write by distraction' (p. 139). What she means by this is that she finds it helpful to divert her 'gaze' away from its intended object, to avoid the fatal consequence that would come about if she achieved the feat of actually 'capturing' this object (p. 139). It is only through this process of 'distraction', she explains, though the avoidance of doing the very thing that one has set out to do, that the unknown, the seemingly unknowable or unthinkable unknown (such as the writing of Clarice Lispector) appears on the horizon: 'We search for one land, we find another' (p. 150).

Portraits of Jacques Derrida

By perpetually promising yet never delivering a point of 'arrival', while at the same time progressing towards tangential or otherwise unrelated 'discoveries', the path taken by Cixous's poetic writing appears to have much in common with Derrida's concept of *différance* (where 'meaning', or the signified, is perpetually deferred in an endless chain of difference). In brief, *différance* is a neologism created by Derrida. It is a homonym in French with the word *différence* (difference); it is also closely related to two other homonyms, *différer* (to differ) and *différé* (deferred). *Différance* can thus be thought of as a concept that brings together the sense of 'to differ' (to be different from) and the sense of 'to defer' (to hold something in a state of abeyance). A simple example of what this means can be found if one looks up a word (or signifier) in a dictionary. One does not find the 'meaning' (or the signified) of the word, as such, but merely a collection of other words (other signifiers), which in turn can be looked up elsewhere in the dictionary, which in turn leads to a further set of words (signifiers), which in turn . . . and so on. Derrida's concept of *différance* therefore exposes the fallacy of the claim implicit in Western philosophy that some kind of ultimate truth, or 'transcendental signified', can be discovered, if only (*à la* Descartes or Hegel) one is able to formulate an appropriately rigorous philosophical methodology.[5] However, this supposed similarity between Cixous's poeticism and Derrida's *différance*, like the apparent evidence of Cixous engaging in a 'deconstruction' of binary opposites at the beginning of 'Sorties',[6] should not be taken as an indication that Cixous and Derrida's approaches are one and the same. As Cixous remarks to Mireille Calle-Gruber, while she has 'a very great proximity with Derrida' (*Rootprints*, p. 80), while there are 'a series of fertile coincidences' and 'connections' between her writing and that of Derrida:

> What strikes me with him is precisely to what extent he is different from me ... It's as if, coming from very far away, having covered the same path in the same direction for millennia, parallel, sometimes moving apart, sometimes coming together ... there were the trace in us, each one on our own side, of the long path.   (p. 81)

The difference between them, Cixous adds, can be seen in the (by her own admission, overly simplified) account she gives of the different approaches she and Derrida take to the question of death. For Cixous, 'death is past. It has already taken place'; in the case of Derrida: 'death awaits him ... he is expecting death in the future' (p. 82). One of them accepts the reality of death and moves on; the other is always seemingly in the shadow of death. Therefore, if one accepts this simplification, it can be argued that there is a certain celebration of life, a certain vivacity in Cixous's writing that is not always present in the writing of Derrida. Though once again it must be stressed that this is a simplification made in order to illustrate what is in actuality a highly complex and productive relationship, the contrast between the two writers is wonderfully illustrated in the difference between Cixous and Derrida's contributions to their shared 1998 text, *Voiles (Veils)*.[7] Cixous's short piece, 'Savoir' (pp. 1–16), playfully hovers between fiction, memoir and poetry. 'Savoir' details the circumstances surrounding Cixous's recent operation to 'cure' her myopia, as well as the strange sense of loss and nostalgia Cixous then encounters for her 'secret non-seeing' (p. 16; see also Chapter 6). Derrida's text, 'A Silkworm of One's Own' (pp. 17–108), is in part a response to 'Savoir'; it is also a personal meditation on certain philosophical and theological themes. A much longer, more 'serious' piece than 'Savoir', 'A Silkworm of One's Own' twists and turns in typically Derridean convoluted patterns around its chosen subject (with, unlike 'Savoir', frequent recourse to textual authority and scholarly notes). Cixous's 'Savoir' is content to let its subject matter wander freely, to 'escape' from its author. Derrida's 'A Silkworm of One's Own', on the other hand, reads (in part) like an attempt to 'gather' together and 'plant' its various strands and ideas (if only so it can 'justify' the comments it is making). One is 'poetic'; the other 'philosophical'.

Cixous's recent *Portrait de Jacques Derrida en Jeune Saint Juif* (*Portrait of Jacques Derrida as a Young Jewish Saint*) offers another, striking example of the proximity/difference between their work.[8] *Portrait de Jacques Derrida* emerges from the afterglow of 'A Silkworm of One's Own', as well as 'H. C. Pour la vie, c'est à dire': Derrida's 127-page tribute to Cixous in the collection of texts (from an academic conference devoted to Cixous) published in *Hélène Cixous, croisées d'une œuvre*.[9] Cixous's 'response' to Derrida is to create a wonderfully playful, ironic, tongue-in-cheek text, one that indulges in what appears to be a respectfully wry parody of Derrida's own style, with particular reference to Derrida's 1991 autobiographical text 'Circonfession' ('Circumfession').[10] In the title of his review of *Portrait de Jacques Derrida* for the French left-wing newspaper *Libération* – 'Cixous déride Derrida' – Eric Loret suggests that Cixous 'brightens' or 'cheers up' Derrida.[11] Cixous does this quite literally at various points in the text: highlighting words, or parts of words, in blue and orange type, and then adding her own handwritten marginal comments or notes (see pp. 15, 17, 23, 31, 43, 67, 75, 86, 93). The result is both a textual commentary and a work of visual art. Transcending the boundaries of genre *Portrait de Jacques Derrida* is part essay, part poem.[12]

Portrait de Jacques Derrida en Jeune Saint Juif also serves to shed more light on Cixous and Derrida's common Algerian and Jewish heritage. For Cixous, Jewishness and the poetic connect in two ways. The first of these, as she notes in her seminar at the Centre de Recherches en Etudes Féminines, is the connection between Jewishness and exile, Jewishness and a failure to 'belong'. Speaking of a passage from 'Poem of the End', in which the Russian poet Marina Tsvetayeva (who was not herself Jewish) declares, 'In this most Christian of worlds | all poets are Jews', Cixous comments:

> For Tsvetayeva, all indications are that something of a Jew is in every poet or that every poet is Jewish. The point has nothing to do with religion but with what it means poetically 'to be Jewish'. She suggests that we are better off as wandering Jews, belonging where we cannot belong. (*Readings*, p. 150)[13]

As was discussed in Chapter 1, because of their common French-Algerian and Jewish backgrounds, Cixous sees that she and Derrida have what she describes to Mireille Calle-Gruber as 'a foreign relationship to the French language' (*Rootprints*, p. 84). This 'foreign relationship' does not so much 'determine' as mould and shape the concerns of their writing: to be a poet, to be Jewish, is to be a political outsider (see, for example, Cixous's *Un K. incompréhensible: Pierre Goldman*, discussed in Chapter 3).[14] However, while keeping this political impulse in mind, Cixous also draws on literary and cultural senses of Jewishness – on Jewish texts, philosophies and traditions (although not, it must be admitted, to the extent that Derrida does). In the interview conducted for this present book, Cixous displays a certain initial reluctance regarding the question of her 'Jewish heritage'. In the end, however, she admits to the fact that her 'secret memory . . . is certainly impregnated with Jewish traces', adding that these traces 'belong to the poetical force' that emerges from 'a certain practice of reading which is *highly* developed in Jewish culture' (see Chapter 6). Specifically, Cixous compares her poetic practice of thinking and writing 'the unknown' with the countless generations' worth of scholarship and commentary that have been devoted to the study of the Talmud (the primary source of Jewish religious law). As Cixous tells Mireille Calle-Gruber, what is remarkable about the Talmud is that 'one can neither learn it nor know it, one can only read it, study it and interpret it' (*Rootprints*, p. 56). Cixous sees an analogy in this practice of Talmudic scholarship with the practice of her own writing. As she explains in the interview in this present book, in her writing, as in the Talmud: 'There's no conclusive version, there are a hundred versions. And this is most important. Now, when I look at anything that happens in reality, any kind of event, I want a hundred versions of it' (see Chapter 6). The manner in which Cixous approaches the creation of her writing, she claims, is the same manner in which a scholar approaches a reading of the Talmud. Both are faced with an 'infinite' book (*Rootprints*, p. 56), both know that the truth of their particular book will always elude them, both continue in their reading or writing of this book for this very reason (in fact, the connection is even closer than this analogy might initially suggest – as will be seen in Chapter 5, for Cixous the act of reading and the act of writing cannot be separated from each other). In the end, as Cixous explains in another interview, it is a matter 'of writing the saga of all the efforts to conquer what you will never conquer'.[15] This commitment to the act of reading or writing a circular, unending, 'unfinishable' book (a commitment to writing that does not 'arrive') is perhaps the most crucial component in Cixous's understanding of what it means to be a 'poet'. As Cixous remarks in 'The Last Painting or the Portrait of God', the movement of the poetic is towards the future, in the direction of 'tomorrow' (p. 113). An artist paints a picture of potentiality: 'one paints what will be, one paints "the imminence of"' (p. 113). A poet (or Talmudist) performs a similar operation with the medium of language: 'I call "poet" any writer, philosopher, author of plays, dreamer, dreamer of dreams, who uses life as a time of "approaching"' (p. 114).

The eternity of the instant

The genesis, the pre-birth of writing holds a special fascination for Cixous. As she explains in 'Writing blind': 'My business is to translate our emotions into writings. First we feel. Then I write. The act of writing engenders the author. I write the genesis that occurs before the author' (p. 143). In another recent essay, 'Without end, no, State of drawingness, no, rather: The Executioner's taking off', Cixous confesses that what she desires most of all is 'the beforehand of a book ... the abundance of leaves before the pages ... The to-be-in-the-process of writing.'[16] In an observation that is left by the translator in the original French, Cixous then asks why it is that the gerund has been lost in French: '*Le vrai temps de ce texte est le gérondif* [The gerund is the true tense of this text]' (p. 20). The gerund, recognizable in English by the addition of the '-ing' suffix to the stem of a verb, is the tense that is used to indicate when one is speaking of an action *as it is happening* (that is to say, when the action being spoken of is 'in-the-process of'). This is the tense of Cixous's theatrical writing (the immediacy she speaks of in 'From the Scene of the Unconscious ...'). It is also the tense of Cixous's poetic thinking and writing (the 'time of "approaching"' she recommends in 'The Last Painting or the Portrait of God').

In the opening gambit of her essay 'In October 1991 . . .', Cixous remarks: 'I like being in the present; am interested in what's in process'.[17] What Cixous calls in this essay 'the eternity of the instant' (p. 35) encapsulates an immense range of emotions, details, comings and goings, all of which take place in an infinitesimally small moment of time. As she notes elsewhere, in trying to write the present, she is attempting a similar task to that of a painter who tries to replicate the motion of 'light' on a static canvas or screen: 'what a painter as poet is trying to paint is movement and what disappears . . . It is exactly the same in writing. What I do is just to deal with what is appearing and disappearing *in the same moment.*'[18] The way Cixous deals with 'this structure of appearance-disappearance' (p. 340), she adds, is by writing things down *as they happen*:

> the moment a something flashes . . . I try to note *it* down because
> I know that five minutes later its itness will have vanished totally,
> even from my memory. It's not because I am a miser, it's simply
> because this is absolutely exceptional: it's something that has been
> given, which is irreplaceable and if I don't make the effort to note it
> down immediately it's as if it never had happened.   (p. 341)

However, it must be said, as Cixous explains to Mireille Calle-Gruber, no matter how great her desire to 'write in the present' may be, Cixous is also aware that the task she has set herself is an impossible one: it is only ever possible to write 'after the present', at a time when the present has already become past (*Rootprints*, p. 78). Cixous addresses this problem in the first of her *Three Steps*, 'The School of Death'. On the one hand, she reflects: 'Writing is this effort not to obliterate the picture, not to forget' (p. 7). That is to say, writing is an act of memorialization, an act in which one strives to preserve what has been, what is, and what will 'five minutes later' be no more. One can see 'this effort . . . not to forget' in Cixous's decision to finally write about her mother, and her mother's memories and stories, in recent texts such as *Osnabrück*, *Le jour où je n'étais pas là* and *Les Rêveries de la femme sauvage* (see Chapters 3 and 6). It is the same impulse that also drives and comforts the Shakespeare of the *Sonnets*. In the most well known of his sonnets, sonnet 18 ('Shall I compare thee to a summer's day?'), Shakespeare is faced with the knowledge that the elegance and beauty of the young man is merely transient and passing ('summer's lease hath all too short a date'). Therefore, having set out the fact that the young man's physical beauty will not last, Shakespeare suggests that writing might be employed as a means of preservation and remembrance:

> But thy eternal summer shall not fade,
> Nor lose possession of that fair thou ow'st,
> Nor shall Death brag thou wand'rest in his shade,
> When in eternal lines thou grow'st.
>> So long as men can breathe or eyes can see,
>> So long lives this, and this gives life to thee.

Of course, the irony is that while this sonnet, this instance of writing, is still with us, the identity of the young man about whom it was written has been irredeemably lost. Writing, therefore, while it can preserve certain aspects of a person or story, cannot hold on to everything. Something is always going to be lost in the transition from life to text, from present to past. This state of affairs is succinctly expressed by one of Cixous's many neologisms, *oublire*, which is a word created to indicate that when we read we also forget (*oublire* is a 'portmanteau word' made up from the combination of *oublier*, to forget, and *lire*, to read).[19] Consequently, as Cixous observes in *Three Steps*, as well as being a (partly doomed) attempt to hold on to things, writing is also about letting go, about coming to the acceptance that things will pass and about celebrating this passing: 'Writing is learning to die. It's learning not to be afraid ... to live at the extremity of life' (p. 10). It is the knowledge that even writing will come to an end, the understanding that comes with 'knowing that the present passes' ('From the Scene of the Unconscious ...', p. 7), that helps Cixous avoid the fatal consequence of actually capturing or preserving the present (of trapping the present, forever, as if it were set in stone). The impossibility of writing the present allows for the formation of a non-possessive, non-grasping, lovingly 'feminine' approach to the instant. In tones that recall her earlier writing about achieving the proper distance or approach to the other, Cixous notes in 'Writing blind' that it is not her intention 'to keep' the instant; on the contrary, she adds: 'I write to feel. I write to touch the body of the instant with the tips of words' (p. 146). Cixous brushes against the instant. Her texts are like the ends of the fingers of a hand that is trailing along the back of a passing cat: not grasping, not holding on, but alive and tingling with the electricity of the moment. It is this connection with and valuing of the transitory, the passing, the unknowable that gives Cixous's writing its unique and luminous poetic intensity.

The School of Dreams

Cixous's writing is at its most intensely poetic in its use of and connection with dreams. Often, the first thing Cixous does upon awaking is to write down her dreams, to 'preserve' a little something, a remembrance of the dream before it all evaporates and disappears. Since Freud's *The Interpretation of Dreams*, the link has been made between the world of dreams and the unconscious. For Cixous, the two of them come together in the creation of metaphors. Cixous's writing has always been richly metaphorical. As she observes to Mireille Calle-Gruber: 'For me, the origin of the metaphor is the unconscious ... for a long time I have permitted myself to use the writing of dreams to conduct a certain research in writing' (*Rootprints*, p. 27). The descriptions Cixous gives of what she finds and values in her dreams might be construed along the lines of a personal, individual equivalent to the 'possession' and '*démoïsation*' she experiences in her writing for the theatre (see 'From the Scene of the Unconscious ...', p. 13). In her dream writing, she says: 'A force that does not belong to me goes through me. A force that I am not recounts my story to me' (*Rootprints*, p. 27). Whether she is awake or dreaming, this force operates in the same way, produces the same effects: 'It truly comes from the inside. I do not see how one can write otherwise than by letting oneself be carried away on the back of those funny horses that are metaphors' (p. 28). Dreams are exhilarating, liberating. Cixous's dream writing emerges from the knowledge that she is not in control of the writing. As Cixous explains: 'one must leave oneself go. One must not be afraid ... one sets off, without brakes, without harness' (p. 39). The dreams take over, set the agenda, choose the subjects, the images, the relations, the directions the text will follow. In dream writing, Cixous observes in *Three Steps*, one has to face up to and will be freed by the fact that some other force is 'the driver' of the text: 'The book writes itself, and if by chance the person opposite should ask you what you are writing, you have nothing to say since you don't know' (p. 100).

It is arguably in the dream world, in Cixous's dream writing, that one finds the closest correspondence with the imagined form or style of *écriture féminine*. Cixous discusses dreams at great length and with great enthusiasm in *Three Steps*. In her writing about dreams one can see the appearance (and disappearance) of the unknown, the unexpected, the elusive and passing instant. Cixous argues that the beauty of dreams is that they do not operate within the normal constraints of textual rules. The concepts of time, order and sequential progression do not apply. As Cixous remarks: 'There is no transition: you wake up in the dream in the other world, on the other side; there is no passport, no visa but this extreme familiarity with extreme strangeness' (p. 80). The instantaneous nature of the transition into the dream world means that dreams can become the space of the truly other, a space where 'the feeling of foreignness is absolutely pure' (p. 80). If one is open to the 'pure' foreign, Cixous contends, then the transition in the dream world, though it is an act of total displacement, is achieved without trauma, without fear. As will be seen in more detail in the next chapter, Cixous's 'reading' of events in the dream world has strong affinities with the way in which she approaches her writing and reading of a text. In both cases Cixous stresses the seemingly limitless possibilities and the sense of freedom that comes about with the total, instantaneous immersion into extreme otherness that she associates with dreams: 'In the text, as in dreams, there is no entrance. I offer this as a test to all apprentice-writers: if you are marking time you are not yet there. In the text, as in the dream, you're right there' (p. 81). For Cixous, it can be said that (like the pre-Symbolic, 'innocent' non-space of the Real) dreams represent an impossible, unobtainable, but highly desirable ideal. As she notes in *Three Steps*, in committing to the act of writing, to the state of being a writer, one must behave as if one is travelling to 'a foreign country' – even to the extent of becoming 'foreigners inside our own families' (p. 21). What this means, Cixous explains, is that while she is writing (just as when she is dreaming), all other considerations, personal and professional, are left behind: 'I escape myself, I uproot myself, I am a virgin; I leave from my own house and I don't return' (p. 21). Her books emerge from her own experiences, dreams, research, conversations, but it is only when she totally immerses herself in the process of writing that the book itself can be written. For Cixous, there are no half-measures in writing. If one leaves a book halfway through its composition, it is like waking up halfway through a dream: something, inevitably, will be lost. Likewise, when Cixous 'reads' a dream, she does so in such a way that she does not interfere with the dream – she leaves the dream's foreignness, its otherness, intact. As Cixous notes, it is important to remember that 'there is no explanation' that can be profitably made of a dream; on the contrary: 'any explanation would destroy the magic' (p. 81). Seemingly in deliberate contrast to the approach to dreams taken by Freud, Cixous remarks: 'Like plants, dreams have their enemies, plant lice that devour them. The dream's enemy is interpretation' (p. 107). What this implies for Cixous's practice as a reader, for her work as a literary critic, is discussed in the next chapter.

Chapter 5

Cixous on others: others on Cixous

> Writing forms a passageway between two shores.
>
> (Three Steps, p. 3)

This chapter will examine Hélène Cixous's role as a reader and teacher of literature; it will also look at some of the ways in which Cixous's own texts have been read by others. Because of the rich 'intertextuality' of most of Cixous's writing, rather than catalogue all of Cixous's readings of and allusions to other writers it will examine some of the ways in which Cixous reads (and is 'read by') the writing of Clarice Lispector. Although it is a number of years since Cixous last wrote or spoke at length about Clarice Lispector, Lispector's writing is still one of the major – perhaps even *the* major – outside factors to have had an impact/influence on Cixous's writing. Some aspects of the impact/influence of Lispector's writing on Cixous have been discussed in previous chapters (see esp. Chapter 3). This examination of Cixous's reading practice will concentrate on how Lispector's writing was 'read' in Cixous's seminar at the Centre de Recherches en Etudes Féminines.

'Feminine' reading

Cixous is extremely interested in what happens when we read a text. For Cixous, writing only truly comes to life when a dialogue or interchange is established with the act of reading. As she explains in *Three Steps*: 'Writing and reading are not separate, reading is a part of writing. A real reader is a writer. A real reader is already on the way to writing' (p. 21). Reading is a vital part of the 'genesis' or 'pre-birth' of her writing. Cixous's readings of texts, the approaches she takes when she speaks and writes about the writing of others, can thus be seen as another piece in the jigsaw of *écriture féminine*. It is in the 'femininity' of a certain practice of reading texts, just as much as in the 'femininity' of writing them, that the revolution-in-language which Cixous calls for in 'Sorties' can and will take place (see Chapter 2). Cixous sees reading as a liberating and transgressive experience, one in which it is possible to step outside and exceed the boundaries of the dominant 'masculine' order: 'Reading is eating the forbidden fruit, making forbidden love ... Reading is doing everything we want and "on the sly" ' (*Three Steps*, pp. 21–2). Reading is also a complex and delicate balancing act, requiring much care, skill and thought on the part of the reader. As Cixous comments at the commencement of the transcripts from her seminar at the Centre de Recherches en Etudes Féminines collected in *Reading with Clarice Lispector*, there are a wide variety of ways in which the strangeness or otherness of a text can be listened to and explored. Cixous's description of these different possible approaches to a text can be tentatively put forward as the outline of a 'feminine' practice of reading:

> When we read a text, we are either read by the text or we are in the text. Either we tame a text, we ride on it, we roll over it, or we are swallowed up by it, as by a whale. There are thousands of possible relations to a text, and if we are in a nondefensive, nonresisting relationship, we are carried off by the text. This is mainly the way it goes. But then, in order to read, we need to get out of the text. We have to shuttle back and forth incessantly. We have to try all possible relations with a text. At some point, we have to disengage ourselves from the text as a living ensemble, in order to study its construction, its techniques, and its texture.   (p. 3)

A book has a hundred windows

From the outset of her career as a writer and literary critic (with the publication of *Le Prénom de Dieu* [*The First Name of God*] and her doctorat d'Etat, *The Exile of James Joyce*),[1] Cixous has been interested in what she describes as 'so-called experimental writers' – writers who 'revolutionize' and 'turmoil language' in new and 'adventurous' ways.[2] Cixous explains in *Three Steps* that she feels as if she is drawn to a very particular type (or types) of text: 'I obey the call of certain texts . . . I am rejected by others' (p. 5). The texts . . . that appeal to her are possessed of many 'different voices', yet, she adds, 'they all have one voice in common . . . a certain music I am attuned to' (p. 5). Cixous expands on this theme in her 'Inter Views' with Mireille Calle-Gruber: 'The books that I love are not masterful narratives but journals of experiences. They are books that have recorded, and indeed left intact, *the emergence* of an experience that has been located or noticed for the first time' (*Rootprints*, p. 57). Her interests as a reader are the same as her interests as a poetic writer: the emergent, the approaching, the being-in-the-process of (see Chapter 4). These interests mean that Cixous will often work on the fringes of texts, on notebooks, fragments, drafts, manuscripts, letters, diaries – what Gérard Genette refers to as 'pre-texts' (the texts that come before the published text).[3] In the case of Kafka, for instance, Cixous finds herself turning to his 'journals and correspondence' more often than she does to his fiction (*Rootprints*, p. 57). With other writers, however, such as (in particular) Clarice Lispector, Cixous finds that the economy of 'approaching' is present throughout the oeuvre, it can be found in whichever text (or pre-text) one chooses to read. With the writing of Clarice Lispector, she explains: 'one never arrives at a place, one always strives towards it' (*Reading with C. L.*, p. 63). Because of this 'striving', (much like Cixous's own writing) Lispector's writing does not take kindly to being quoted in small, bite-size segments. Unless passages are quoted at length, or in their entirety, most of the momentum, interplay and music of the writing will be lost: 'In Clarice's texts it is impossible to make a cut. The whole of her text is so necessary, she has descended so exactly to the place of writing that no matter where we are, we are always in the middle of writing' (*Three Steps*, p. 133). In *Reading with Clarice Lispector*, Cixous illustrates the difficulties Lispector's writing presents to the reader who wishes to talk about one of her texts with reference to Lispector's remarkable 1973 novel *Agua viva* (*The Stream of Life*).[4] Cixous remarks in her seminar on this text that '*Agua viva* is a text that can produce resistance and anguish in the reader because it is governed by a different order. One could say that from the point of view of a classical order, it is completely disorganized' (*Reading with*

C. L., p. 11). There is no gradual build-up, no gentle fading into the text. *The Stream of Life* opens with a moment of immediacy, pace and movement: 'It's with such intense joy. It's such an hallelujah. "Hallelujah", I shout, an hallelujah that fuses with the darkest human howl of the pain of separation but is a shout of diabolical happiness. Because nobody holds me back any more' (p. 3). Dizzyingly, breathlessly, Lispector's text runs on ahead. It flows with incredible speed and continuity, with barely a ripple, or a word out of place. Cixous describes *The Stream of Life* as 'living water': it is a text, she says, that is possessed not of 'a narrative', but 'an organic order' (*Reading with C. L.*, p. 15). *The Stream of Life*, she contends, 'escapes the first rule of text. It is not linear, not formally constructed' (p. 15). Cixous ponders as to whether or not Lispector's text is in actuality 'readable' (p. 15) – that is, readable on a literary critical level (within the context of the seminar). Perhaps it is, she concludes, but: 'One may have to find other modes, other ways of approaching it' (p. 15).

The first thing to note about the 'other modes' or 'ways' Cixous adopts in her approach to texts such as *The Stream of Life* is that there is no fixed point at which a reading ought to begin. It is only convention that tells us we should start on the first page of a book and work our way through, plodding from one page to the next, until we reach the end. In contrast, Cixous writes and reads books in such a way that any point in the text serves just as well as any other for the 'first' page. For instance, in the attempt to tell Promethea's story, one of the narrators of *Promethea*, 'I', is forced to admit that 'each page I write could be the first page of the book' (p. 14). She describes *Promethea* as 'a day-by-day book', explaining that 'each day, the one happening now, is the most important day' (p. 14). *Promethea*, therefore, is a book that cannot close or finish because it never gets beyond the moment of conception: 'This whole book is composed of first pages' (p. 15). Likewise, as a reader, Cixous feels that she is freed from the conventions of linear, sequential narrative. It is only if one steps outside of these conventions, she argues, it is only if one admits that there are other ways of approaching and moving through a text, that the full spectrum of potential and possibility within the text is revealed: 'A book does not have a head and feet. It does not have a front door. It is written from all over at once, you enter it through a hundred windows' ('Writing blind', p. 145). It needs to be stressed that Cixous is not advocating complete anarchy in her reading practice. She does not wish to do away with 'method' entirely. Rather, she is suggesting that a reader ought to be open to the multiplicity of approaches each text individually and uniquely requires: 'A capacity for improvisation should mark a reading process that could be qualified as feminine and that is one of improvisation as well as logic' (*Reading with C. L.*, p. 4). This 'improvisation' extends to the links Cixous makes between texts and writers. When Cixous reads a text, the links she makes between it and other texts by the same or other writers are formed out of what these texts have in common ethically, thematically, poetically, rather than out of the coincidence or accident that they share the same historical or cultural context. In a way, for Cixous all the writers she reads are 'contemporary' with each other.

In addition to the 'sequence' or 'order' in which a text is read, in a 'feminine' practice of reading the distance between the reader and the text has to be thought through, the line of sight needs to be constantly focused and refocused as the text moves in and out of view. There is no 'correct' distance from which one can approach a text. Like a wave moving through water, or the interference pattern one sees in a beam of light that has passed through narrow, parallel slits, a text has its peaks and troughs, its points of brightness and clarity, as well as its points of darkness, its blind spots. As Cixous explains in *Reading with Clarice Lispector*: 'If one looks at a thing too closely, it disappears; if one is too far, it also disappears until the moment when it reappears. There is a constant passage to the infinite through proximity of distance' (p. 112). It is neither in proximity nor in distance, but in a combination of the two that a text needs to be read. Consequently, Cixous explains in her 'Conversations' with the members of the seminar, she finds it necessary to take up a variety of reading positions (close up, far away, somewhere in-between): 'I like to work like an ant, crawling the entire length of a text and examining all its details, as well as like a bird that flies over it, or like one of Tsvetayeva's immense ears, listening to its music' (p. 148). By looking at the text close up, as if through a microscope, Cixous can see the details, the minutiae of the text come into view. As she notes in 'The Last Painting or the Portrait of God', she takes this approach to writing 'because I am near-sighted' (p. 109). It is due to her 'nearsightedness', she argues, that she 'looks at things from very, very close up. Seen through my eyes, little things are very big. Details are my kingdoms' (p. 109). With prolonged exposure to such close proximity, changes occur. When the eyes are lifted up from the page, the world is altered: 'I owe some of the most fantastical hallucinatory experiences of my child-hood to my extreme nearsightedness: vanishing streets, substitu-tions, metaphorization and metonymization of the world and people' (*Rootprints*, p. 89). No matter how productive the experi-ence may seem to be, if one focuses too intently on the minute details of a text there is much that will be missed. Therefore, as well as looking at the text through a 'microscope', one also needs to look at it through something akin to a telescope. One needs to look at the text as if it is a far-off shoreline whose details, though slightly obscured by the distance, gather together to form an image of a collective whole. As Cixous observes in *Reading with Clar-ice Lispector*, it is important to remember that 'the life of the text' consists not only of 'a quantity of small units', but also that these units come together to form 'a general ensemble' (p. 100). For this reason, she adds: 'A text has to be read in its entirety. It is only afterward that one can look at its fingernails, as in times when we are in love' (p. 100). That is to say, the full significance of indivi-dual details can only be understood when placed in the context of the whole. While it is true to say that words or images signify when looked at in isolation, this effect is amplified, multiplied if one considers them in the context of all the other words and images in the text: 'It is only in the aftereffect that things fall into place and fragments of meaning emerge' (p. 104). Just as, Cixous contends, one would not dream of cutting 'a symphony into little pieces' (p. 100), the overall integrity, the organic interconnected-ness of the written text needs to be respected, needs to be given room in which to express itself. One must allow meaning to settle, like sediment, upon the conscious and unconscious mind of the reader. As Cixous explains: 'Because a text is printed, one often

forgets that it is mobile ... One should always bring back the
movement of the text, the fact that meaning runs along it like music
that reaches us only once it has been fully played' (p. 100).

Reading with Hélène Cixous

Cixous's seminars at the Centre de Recherches en Etudes Féminines have been running since 1980. Verena Andermatt Conley's
two edited selections of translations are taken from the first five
years of the seminar.[5] *Reading with Clarice Lispector* and *Readings:
The Poetics of Blanchot, Joyce, Kafka, Kleist, Lispector, and Tsvetayeva*
offer invaluable and illuminating passages of commentary by
Cixous, giving the reader a feel for what Conley describes as
Cixous's 'litanic style, in which a pedagogical discourse is mixed
with that of a poet' (*Reading with C. L.*, p. ix). As an introduction to
Cixous's approach to literary criticism, these two texts are highly
recommended. However, by their very nature, one thing that is
omitted from these texts is the presence of the other voices in
the seminar, the other points of view, the other approaches to the
texts, the others who are present, physically, in the room. In this
respect, the selection of translations collected in *Writing Differences:
Readings from the Seminar of Hélène Cixous* provides an interesting companion piece and counterpoint to Conley's two texts (ideally, all
three books should be read together). Two of the ten 'readings'
in *Writing Differences* are by Cixous.[6] Two of the other readings, by
Pierre Salesne and Sarah Cornell, are of Cixous.[7] The other six
readings which these texts 'bookend' (if one reads the book sequen-
tially, that is) are all, arguably, inspired by Cixous (that is to say,
to one degree or another they carry traces of Cixous's influence
while, at the same time, reflecting the individual writer's own
thoughts, emotions and motivations). *Writing Differences* 'concludes'
with 'Conversations' (pp. 141–54), a text in which Cixous and the
other contributors to the volume discuss the kind of work, the kind
of reading, that is done in the seminar, as well as what being a
participant in the seminar means to them. Though it is not a transcript from the seminar (it is the edited highlights of two conversations that took place at Cixous's home in Paris in April 1986),

'Conversations' arguably provides something akin to a microcosm or simulacrum of the seminar.

Listening to the voice of the other

In the seminar at the Centre de Recherches en Etudes Féminines, the first thing one notices is the silence. Someone, perhaps Cixous, perhaps someone else, is speaking. Everyone else in the room is listening, perhaps noting down a point, perhaps looking at something in the text being discussed. The quality of the listening is intense. It can feel as if the words of the person speaking, and the words of the text they are speaking about, are all there is. There is no interruption. Each person speaks for their allotted time. When the speaker has finished they return to their place and someone else takes their turn. There is little discussion of what is being said – or, rather, discussion occurs silently, in a dialogue between the speaker's words and the listener's thoughts. Another noticeable aspect is the range of spoken accents. The participants come from all over the world. Though French is the adopted language of expression, the languages of the texts – English, German, Brazilian, Russian (and so on) – are each given due space in which to be heard. This multilingualism is important because, as Cixous observes:

> One of the efforts we make is to be transgrammatical, the way one could say transgressive. It is not that we despise grammar, but we do not have to obey it absolutely; and we have to work to some degree on degrammaticalization. From this point of view, it is good to work on foreign texts – Clarice Lispector's, James Joyce's and others' – because they displace our relation to grammar.
>
> (*Reading with C. L.*, p. 4)

This 'displacement' of grammar can be seen, in one respect, as a continuation of Cixous's 'foreign relationship' with French. It is a political choice of language, one in which she works towards a 'feminine' practice of writing and reading that is outside the 'masculine' signifying economy, a practice of reading that is not, as she puts it in one of her early texts, 'subjected to the gramma-r wolf' (*Coming to Writing*, p. 22). However, one can also say that this economy of 'degrammaticalization' informs, facilitates and enriches the relationship between the reader and the other (that is, the other who speaks in a 'foreign' text).

Cixous makes the observation in 'Conversations' that when she is immersed in the many languages of the seminar, she occasionally gets the sensation that what is occurring is in some way 'replying to the curse of Babel' (p. 146). As she explains: 'The biblical curse was finding oneself prey to a multiplicity of languages but I see it as a blessing to be in the midst of so many languages. For languages say different things. And our multiple collectivity makes these differences – this infinite enrichment – apparent to us' (p. 146). Cixous considers that her 'most refined work' is performed in her exploration of what happens below the 'surface' of a text, at the level of consciousness where, if one looks closely enough, if one listens intently enough, one can 'perceive a different kind of text in the text itself' (*Reading with C. L.*, pp. 100–1). It is at this level, she argues, that 'one can speak of a textual unconscious. A text says something very different from what it is supposed to say or thinks that it says' (p. 101). However, this 'textual unconscious' is extremely sensitive to the shifts that occur in all levels of language when a text is translated. Taken outside of its original language, given a different tongue with which to speak, 'part of the reality of a text' is lost in translation (pp. 100–1). As a counterbalance to this negative effect, the many languages represented in the seminar, as well as Cixous's own polyglottism, are invaluable aids in the production of a respectful, 'feminine' reading of a text. Cixous can read Kafka, Kleist, and others, in the original German. Shakespeare and Joyce she explores in English. Cixous studied Russian so that she could read the poetry of Tsvetayeva. She learned Portuguese so that she would not needlessly miss even the slightest nuance in the writing of Clarice Lispector. This is the first stage, but the work of 'understanding' a 'foreign' text does not end there. As Cixous observes in 'Conversations', once she has read these non-French-speaking writers, she then tries to 'preserve the essence of each individual language as it passes from one language to the other' (p. 146). It is only by doing this, Cixous explains, by taking each text in hand and deliberately trying not 'to *reduce* it to French', that one makes it possible for the other to come into view:

The work we do is a work of love, comparable to the work of love
that can take place between two human beings. To understand the
other, it is necessary to go in their language, to make the journey
through the other's imaginary. For you are strange to me. In the
effort to understand, I bring you back to me, compare you to me.
I translate you in me. And what I note is your difference, your
strangeness. At that moment, perhaps, through recognition of my
own differences, I might perceive something of you.   (p. 146)

Reading the other

Eventually, as is the case with her writing in other genres, Cixous's
reading always returns to the question of the other (the question
of how one can speak about, or approach towards, or listen to,
or read the other). Cixous stresses again and again that the other
is not just important, the other is not just significant, the other is
everything: 'The other in all his or her forms gives me *I*. It is on the
occasion of the other that *I* catch sight of *me*; or that *I* catch *me* at:
reacting, choosing, refusing, accepting. It is the other who makes
my portrait. Always' (*Rootprints*, p. 13; see also Chapter 6). Cixous
learns a number of valuable lessons about the approach to (and
nature of) the other in her reading of Clarice Lispector's writing.
What is required, Cixous observes in *Readings*, what Clarice Lispector shows her, is a sense of 'generosity', the development of
'an active passivity capable of bearing transition and transference'
(p. 47). It is a 'problem', she notes in *Reading with Clarice Lispector*, of
trying 'to write, speak, evoke the other' without doing so 'from ourselves' (p. 143). This 'problem' is a familiar one in Cixous's own
writing. Two examples should suffice to show how Clarice Lispector approaches the 'problem' of the other, as well as what 'solu-
tions' Cixous feels that she finds in Lispector's texts.

The first of these examples concerns a passage from Lispector's
The Stream of Life in which the narrator, briefly, encounters a beautiful man:

I noticed him suddenly and he was so extraordinarily beautiful and
virile a man that I felt a joy of creation. It's not that I wanted him for
myself, just as I don't want for myself the little boy with the hair of
the archangel I saw running after the ball. I just wanted to look. The

> man looked at me for an instant and smiled calmly: he knew how
> beautiful he was and I know that he knew I didn't want him for
> myself. He smiled because he didn't feel threatened.   (p. 52)

Following this 'encounter', the narrator crosses the street and
gets into a taxi. The encounter is brief, intense, it all happens in
an instant. Indeed, as Cixous observes: 'probably nothing of what
can be called "happening" happens here' (*Reading with C. L.*, p. 52).
The narrator and the beautiful man do not touch, do not speak, but
something happens between them, a 'connection' is made. Cixous
works a little on the 'necessary delicacy' of Lispector's 'style' in
this passage (p. 52), comparing it with the style of Flaubert in *L'education sentimentale* (*Sentimental Education*), which Cixous describes
as '*the* manual of French narrative' (p. 53).[8] Cixous sees that these
two writers are 'as far removed from' each other 'as possible'
(p. 53). Flaubert's point of view is that of 'an absolute masculinity',
Lispector is coming from the point of view of 'an absolute femininity' (pp. 53–4). Flaubert's writing is 'tempered by *comme* (like),
because Flaubert is the author of analogy' (p. 54). Flaubert does
not describe things as they are, but as what they are similar to:
he names, appropriates, codifies and fixes the objects on which he
gazes. Lispector, on the other hand, Cixous argues, lets the thing be
itself: she does not interpret, she looks. Speaking of the sentence, 'I
just wanted to look', Cixous remarks: 'That is Clarice's motto. To
look absolutely is not to look at anyone or at anything, but to look
purely' (p. 54). For Cixous, the fact that the man knows '"how
beautiful he was"' can be understood as an epiphany, as the
moment of revelation' (p. 55). There is no 'vulgar narcissism' in
this knowledge (p. 55), she contends, it is more a case of a 'feminine'
relationship to pleasure (see Chapter 2). To illustrate this point,
Cixous describes a scene from a story by Kleist in which 'a boy
who did not know that he was handsome' is told that he is so by
the narrator:

> From then on, the boy loses his beauty. Here [in *The Stream of Life*],
> it is the contrary. The nonappropriating look gives the man the
> pleasure of his own beauty. This pleasure is marked in 'how
> beautiful he was'. He fully indulges in pleasure because no
> implications of seduction or castration are at stake.   (p. 55)

Lispector's narrator is content to let the beautiful man be beautiful. She does not impose or force beauty upon him, she leaves alone and, in leaving alone, she shares in the epiphany of the passing, transient 'encounter' with his beauty. In Cixous's eyes, Lispector's narrator connects with the other by allowing the other to remain so.

The second example of Cixous's reading of Lispector concerns a single sentence from Lispector's short text 'Tanta mansidão' ('Such mansuetude').[9] In 'Tanta mansidão', Cixous explains, 'Clarice writes about being at the window and watching the rain' (*Reading with C. L.*, p. 78). This is all that happens. It is a text about rain, about rain on a window, about rain seen through a window. Cixous is drawn to the simplicity, the sparse economy of Lispector's writing: 'It is this barely writing the rainy aspect of rain that one could call, in our vocabulary, an emanation of femininity' (p. 78). Cixous singles out one sentence in particular that, she feels, exemplifies what it is that Lispector is doing in this text: 'The way rain is not grateful not to be a stone' (quoted on p. 78; trans. by Conley). What is striking for Cixous in this sentence is the way in which the rain does not have to draw on a sense of 'opposition' in order to 'mark' its 'difference' (p. 78). The rain simply is: 'The rain is so much rain that it suffices itself as rain' (p. 78). The difference of the rain is marked purely internally, 'through affirmation' (p. 78). As Cixous explains:

> Clarice's technique consists in ending by saying: 'Rain is'. But in order to say that, she proceeds in a way that resembles negative theology. She begins by saying: 'Rain is not a stone'. We are obliged, the world being what it is, to go through the negative in order to bring about the affirmative, not the positive. The positive would refer us back to the negative.   (p. 79)

Lispector's text allows the rain to be rain, but does not try to understand the rain. She says that the rain *is*, but does not say *what* the rain is. Like the true nature of God, as it is 'understood' in negative theology, the rain remains beyond comprehension. What Cixous finds in Lispector is an approach to the other, and to otherness, that understands the incomprehensibility of the other. 'The supreme statement of love', Cixous explains, 'would be: I do not understand you' (p. 65). Cixous fears nothing more than 'any type of comprehension' (p. 66), to understand the other is to destroy the other – hence her desire to be always in a state of *différance*, 'thinking the unthinkable' (see Chapter 4).[10]

Readings of/with Hélène Cixous

Of the three writers whose names are most often linked together in Anglo-American theoretical discourse under the misleading and damagingly reductive heading of 'French feminism' – that is, Hélène Cixous, Luce Irigaray and Julia Kristeva – Cixous has received the least critical commentary and analysis.[11] For a variety of reasons, while the idea of an *écriture féminine* is widely cited in theoretical and literary critical texts, it is rare to see the discussion move beyond Cixous's texts of the 1970s (see Chapter 1). Toril Moi's chapter on Cixous in her influential 1985 study *Sexual/Textual Politics* (one of the first books to introduce the ideas of 'French feminism' to the English-speaking world), 'Hélène Cixous: An Imaginary Utopia', perhaps spoke for many at the time with its claim that although Cixous's work 'constitutes an invigorating utopian evocation of the imaginative powers of women', it is nevertheless 'marred' by the presence of 'a series of political problems' to which 'the feminist reader of Cixous' will find no satisfactory answer.[12] This critique of Cixous's supposed political naïvety or disinterest is a common theme in many early (and some recent) discussions of Cixous. Considered in the light of what now appears to be the overwhelming evidence to the contrary – especially in Cixous's writing from *L'Indiade* onwards – it is a critique that it is difficult, if not impossible, to sustain (a point that was made very well in Morag Shiach's 1991 study, *Hélène Cixous: A Politics of Writing*).[13] Likewise, it needs to be said that any comparison between Cixous, Irigaray and Kristeva is in one form or another unfair. There are significantly more points of difference than there are points of similarity between these three writers. As was argued previously (see Chapter 4), if a comparison must be made with any of her 'theoretical' contemporaries, then Cixous's writing is arguably closer to Derrida's than anyone else's. This comparison is taken to the extreme in Gayatri Chakravorty Spivak's polemical essay, 'French Feminism in an International Frame', in which, citing what she feels is 'Cixous's faithfulness to, or unquestioning acceptance of, Derrida', Spivak as good as dismisses Cixous as a mere Derridean disciple.[14] Again, this is unfair. As was observed earlier, while they 'are often attracted, interested, questioned, moved or disturbed by the same mysteries' (*Rootprints*, p. 81), there is a world of difference in the approaches Cixous and Derrida take to writing about these topics. Though Spivak would have been unaware of it at the time she was writing, in her seminar at the Centre de Recherches en Etudes Féminines Cixous shows herself to be very far from the position of displaying 'faithfulness' or 'unquestioning acceptance' in her readings of Derrida (see, for example, *Readings*, pp. 89–92). Derrida, likewise, is very far from adopting a superior ('masculine') attitude in his readings of Cixous (see below). In the end, all comparisons are bound to fall short because, as has been argued in this book, Cixous is an impossible writer to pigeonhole. In many respects, Cixous's perceived 'difficulty' as a literary or cultural 'theorist' rests in her insistence that she is first and foremost a writer, a poet, a creator of literary and dramatic texts. In short, because Cixous's writing does not 'fit' with the conventions or expectations of theoretical discourse, she is often passed over in favour of more obviously 'theoretical', eminently quotable writers. In the book-length discussions of Cixous's writing that have appeared in English, Cixous's fiction and theatrical writing have rightly been given pride of place. From the consideration of the theme of 'writing the feminine',[15] to the promotion of 'a politics of writing', to the question of 'authorship, autobiography and love',[16] Cixous's practice as a writer, and the dialogues that take place between Cixous's texts (as well as the texts by others she writes about or alludes to), have been the main points of focus, the primary sources of critical inspiration. This is a trend that looks set to continue. In two of the most recent studies of Cixous to emerge, one chooses to concentrate on Cixous's role as a playwright,[17] the other reads Cixous within the context of contemporary French women's fiction.[18] All of these studies, in one way or another, address the question of *écriture féminine*, but each does so in such a way that *écriture féminine* is understood to be an underlying principle, a guideline that is loosely followed, rather than the be-all and end-all, the alpha and omega of Cixous's writing.

Two of Cixous's most perceptive readers, Jacques Derrida and Mireille Calle-Gruber, illustrate the benefits of approaching Cixous's writing poetically, of immersing oneself in a word, phrase or passage of text and letting it lead one in whatever direction (or directions) it will. For example, consider the excerpt from Derrida's text 'Fourmis' which is included in *Rootprints* (pp. 119–27).[19] Derrida begins with a dream Cixous has had about a grammatically masculine ant (in French, an ant, *une fourmi*, is a feminine noun), 'Fourmis' then weaves its way forward, via La Fontaine's fable of 'La Cigale et la fourmi [The Cicada and the Ant]' (pp. 119–20),[20] the economy of the gift (p. 120), and the etymology of the word 'insect' (pp. 120–2), until it reaches a reading of a passage from Cixous's *FirstDays* (pp. 122–6; see *FirstDays*, pp. 127–8). Derrida works the various elements of his text into and out of each other. Speaking of Cixous's use of the idiomatic expression ' "All the two of them": *tous les deux*' in the passage from *FirstDays*, he remarks:

> Hélène has a genius for making the language speak, down to the most familiar idiom, the place where it seems to be crawling with secrets which give way to thought. She knows how to make it say what it keeps in reserve, which in the process also makes it come out of its reserve. Thus: *tous les deux* can always be heard as *all the 'twos'*, all the couples, the duals, the duos, the differences, all the dyads in the world: each time there's two in the world.   (*Rootprints*, p. 123)

Even in this short excerpt from his text, there is a wealth of detail, allusion and reference taking place as he 'crawls' over Cixous's writing: running hither and thither, picking up words, marking out trails to be followed. For instance, to follow just the one train of thought: although he claims he is 'not in the process of writing a new fable about *la cigale et le fourmi*' (p. 119), the images Derrida evokes of 'keeping something in reserve', and of 'bringing something out of its reserve', do indeed appear to be alluding to and retelling the story of La Fontaine's fable. The cicada lives a life of pure pleasure and stores no food for the winter, the industrious ant (whom the cicada mocks) does the opposite. When winter comes, and food is hard to come by, the cicada approaches the ant and asks to share some food from its 'reserve' – a request which, eventually, the ant grants. La Fontaine's fable is thus a poetic device, a conceit which Derrida uses to draw out the themes of the gift and sexual difference in Cixous's text. Derrida also recognizes the limits of interpretation, especially in 'the difference' in the way in which he and Cixous write about her dream: 'I stride to the interruption of the dream ... I strangle the dream ... Hélène, as for her, lets the gift of the dream breathe in her writing. It is as if her dream were at home there' (p. 125). Derrida, when writing on Cixous, speaks as a reader, an admirer of her 'beautiful and ... mysterious' prose (p. 126).

Mireille Calle-Gruber takes a similarly poetic and creative approach to Cixous's writing. In her 'Portrait of the Writing' (*Rootprints*, pp. 137–76), Calle-Gruber approaches Cixous's writing through a 'triple modality of speaking' in which she attempts to speak 'about', 'with' and 'on' Cixous (pp. 137–8). Analysis, quotation and commentary each take their turn – sometimes separately, sometimes together – before giving way as another mode of writing, another genre appears in the text. Cixous's writing, Calle-Gruber remarks, requires a plurality of readings, a variety of approaches:

> So the critical approach undecides itself on the invitation of works that offer the ruinous and ruiniform writing of a text masking its way, giving voice all over. The cost is exorbitant: not a single point of view that isn't overwhelmed, not a single role play that is not displaced, not a single narrative that is not eccentric; not a single beginning that is not disjointed between Auctor and Actor, between the she-*author* [*auteur-elle*] eternally dropping ink(er), from book to book, and the I-wing [*je-aile*] pursuing a thousand I(s).   (p. 138)

At times, like Derrida's, Calle-Gruber's readings of Cixous cross over (or ignore) the boundary between 'subject' and 'commentary' to become complex and original works of art in their own right – works that may inspire their own corpus of commentary and interpretation (part of an endless, but fascinating chain of writing about/with/on writing). As Calle-Gruber explains in another text, 'Hélène Cixous: Music Forever or Short Treatise on a Poetics for a Story To Be Sung', when looked at for any length of time: 'The Cixousian sentence becomes infinite, unveiling inexplicit signs, unmarked paths, unwritten letters that may pop up at any moment amidst the disjointed pavement of the page.'[21] The infinite possibilities of alterity and otherness are always present in Cixous's writing, so too are they an integral aspect of writing about/with/ on Cixous: 'Strength does not come from preservation (of the same) but from the irruption of alterity. My life comes to me from the other, love is the mainspring of writing: such is the axiom at the heart of the workings of Hélène Cixous's narrative, the secret of her heart's vitality' (*Rootprints*, p. 174). Calle-Gruber's approach to Cixous is to suggest that one should 'sing' her texts with a multiplicity, a polyphony of voices. This multiplicity can take (at least) three forms. One is the word-play and inventiveness displayed in the texts by Derrida, Calle-Gruber and a number of others (Cixous's elliptical writing styles encourage the reader/critic to adopt similar strategies when writing about/with/on her writing). Another is the range of languages, opinions and experiences that are found in Cixous's seminar, or in the proceedings of a conference or colloquium at which her work has been discussed.[22] Yet another, as Cixous indicates in the next chapter, are the interplays and exchanges of voices and ideas that take place in an interview: the moments when one can see 'the other coming out' (see Chapter 6). Mireille Calle-Gruber's 'Portrait of the Writing' can thus be seen as a continuation of the dialogue she and Cixous engage in during their 'Inter Views' in the same book. Derrida's 'Fourmis', an adjunct to his and Cixous's telephone conversations. Likewise, the next chapter in this current book presents another point of view, another perspective on the reading of/with Cixous that has been argued so far.

Chapter 6

Cixous live

The following interview was conducted in English at Cixous's home in Paris, in June 2002. The authors would like to express their thanks to Hélène Cixous for the patience and generosity of her answers.

The word most often used to describe your writing is 'poetic'. The sense of the poetic runs deep, it flies off in many different tangents. For instance, there seems to be a definite affinity between your writing and music. This is partly found in the words themselves, and in the silences that they inhabit: spaces and effects that encourage the reader to listen to the text, to hear the text sing. *Several of your texts have been set to music –* Rouen, la Trentième Nuit de Mai '31 *being perhaps the most recent,*[1] *but there is also the question of metaphorical · and metonymical movements within your texts; they possess, whether they are 'études' or 'symphonies', an organic interconnectedness; there is the presence of the emotional and the lyrical, and an after-effect that is cathartic, evocative, sensual and so on. How important is music to you as a poetic writer?*

It all depends what is meant by 'music'. Because, let's say there are different sorts of music, or meanings of the word 'music'. For instance, one can speak of a body of musical works. That's one thing. Then there's the music of the text, which is something completely different. So the question is a bit ambiguous: 'How important is music to you as a poetic writer?' I would say that the moment you attribute to a writer the poetic quality, music is there: poetry *is* music. Poetry is the music of philosophy, it's the song of philosophy. It's primordial: it begins with the singing of philosophy. So I can't even say it's important, its essential. It's there. It precedes everything. That's one thing. But what kind of music?

That's why I say if you refer to music *as* a body of composed works it's different. If you refer to music as the soul of philosophy, the singing soul of philosophy, then it's everywhere. I can't write without it. It's what carries me. It's like the stream. I imagine that my writing is like all kinds of floating things, leaves, small barks, sails or fish that are carried on a huge stream with which they make a whole – not one, but a whole, an animated whole – and the current which orients, guides, takes a direction, is the musical movement of thinking. And I can't imagine thinking which is not poetical (that is, musical), which is not playing with all the instruments of language. And actually it's that, I think that the key answer is there. You quote the question of metaphorical and metonymical movements – and everything you say is quite pertinent – but I would add to that something which belongs to the idiom. It is the idiomatic aspect of language – for me French (and if I were writing in English it would be the English idiom, the idiomaticity) – which allows for a work to be a huge variation or étude (I agree with that). Inside language the musical resource is the idiom, in a way that one does not always think about, except for poets. It is the fact that language itself plays games, music, gamuts with the fantastic resources of verbal association, of play, not only alliterations, but the play on signifiers, the way it interweaves. Usually, you know, a text is compared to a textile, to a tapestry – which is true, because indeed you have threads running in and out, and it's embroidered – but for me this tapestry is not silent, it's completely musical, echoing, reverberating. And music is not static. Not only does it give impulses, but it also listens to itself and develops a kind of fine, subtle chorus of themes, of light motifs. And of course all this is verbal. But you know, now I think of it, for instance, there's a level of vulgar intuition in the musicity (if I can say so) of language in rap music. I think it's awful because it's so poor, but at the same time it's an intuition that everything you say, if you give it a certain intonation, becomes music. It's vulgar and ridiculous because it's not well developed, but it is a right intuition. Not that everything can become music, but that music is first, music comes first.

So that's one thing. The other thing is also the fact that, without calculating it at all, everything I write has a kind of rhythm, a scansion which is very heterogeneous, sometimes with silences (since you speak about these), sometimes with long measures of writing, sometimes, on the contrary, with very short ones. It alternates between kind of long waves of writing and then, differently, with kinds of little pebbles of writing – and this, I know, is a kind of voice that can be woven with a strictly musical voice. That's why my texts are very often set to music, because musicians feel at home with what I write. For them, I suppose they don't have to listen, to understand the philosophical aspect or depth. What they hear is the music of it, which they translate into another type of annotation. Without difficulty, obviously, because it has happened quite often. But, this is not a formal aspect, because it carries meaning. It's the way thinking goes about through the strength of rhythms. It's a rhythm. Thinking *is* an exercise in rhythm.

There is this beautiful phrase that occurs in a book on Debussy – it was talking about an opera and it said that 'the silences were what allowed the mystery to speak'.

But of course. Silences are most important. Again it's a montage. You can't have only silence. It's *différance*, the way Derrida would say with an 'a'. You can't have a kind of verbal continuity, except if you're totally crazy, it's unbearable (if you had a huge body and flesh of *only* sound). The silence makes the sound and vice versa. But silences have to be arranged in writing. There *are* silences (or there are strengths and beaches which are necessary for the sea to be heard, or for the sky to be seen or observed), but in writing you have to arrange them. For instance, I always strive for blanks and I know that for the printers, and for the publisher [*laughs*], it's a problem, because white blanks use paper for nothing. You see? So it costs money . . . I would like to have many, many white pages, but this is impossible. In the economy of printing they don't like it. It's waste. But for me, this waste is the birthplace of meaning.

Words travel through your texts picking up memories and associations, rather like those little seeds that one always finds after having wandered through a field of long grass. Often by the end of a text one finds that seemingly mundane words acquire an almost spiritual significance: the oranges and apples in Vivre l'orange/To Live the Orange *spring to mind, or the 'Est/Is' that closes* Promethea. *It is this belief in the innate capacity in words to produce the unexpected that is one of the hallmarks of your writing. Where does your fascination with words spring from?*

I don't remember how *Promethea* closes, but let me just point to the fact that 'Est' is both 'Is' and also 'East'. And that's how the language plays: in several directions and at several levels. Now, where does my fascination for words spring from? I would say probably from the first mouthfuls of life, or earfuls [*laughs*], because it's as old as myself. But this is almost biographical. I don't know. I think that I can't remember myself without that. I have the feeling that I was bred on words, brought up on words by my family. Of course, if I didn't have ears, mouth, fingers, etc., to catch the words it wouldn't have worked. But it was there in the beginning. And I remember all my first experiences with words as a baby. All the words I picked up, both in hearing and writing. And the fact that I have always lived the words, as both little magic wands in the huge realm of language and deities: powerful entities that could be misread and misheard – which is *most* important, most important. Misreading and mishearing are also functions which set you on the track of the mysteries of language. Such as, for instance, when you read the word 'e–s–t' and it turns out not to be what you thought, but something else. Words are always not what you thought, but more and more and more and different.

I know that experience of the foreignness, the strangeness, the surprises in words, is something that I probably inherited from my family, because I was born into a multilingual, multilinguistic family where hearing the French of my father, the different Germans of my mother and my grandmother, the Arabic, etc., and the Spanish, all those languages, made me aware of the events that happen in language, with words. It was a surprise for me when I started writing that words would be written in this strange way and be so different from what I heard, and I had this experience several times. When I started learning German at school it was a terrible shock, because written German had *nothing* to do with the spoken German I knew. And of course between those different spaces and levels of language so many, as I said, mishearings or unhearings or transhearings happened, which is the wealth of language. It's like when I'm in my garden, where I write, and at five in the morning the birds start singing. It's very strange, because you realize that there are, let's say, twenty or fifty species of bird in the garden and they don't sing altogether. One starts, and has a very precise song, and then it stops and the song is relayed by another and then by another and by another – it's all different – and they all agree, in a succession, which I think is completely mysterious. Why does this one start and how do they connect and what kind of signs do they give one another so that this one starts and then the other one picks up? It's very extraordinary. Now, regarding words, it's a bit like that. One word calls for another: 'Oran' or 'Orange' calls for 'Iran' and the moment Iran comes in Iran leaves the place for another associated word . . . The work of association *is* mysterious. And it's not mechanical, because it brings in meaning too.

The poetic exists to express beauty, joy and hope; but it is also under pressure to be political, to relate itself to history. As you've just said: we have to think, simultaneously, of both 'the orange' and 'Iran'. Do you see this duality as something that should be valued, or is it something that must be endured?

At first I would be inclined to say that it is something to be valued. Then I would in a second thought say both. Since it is a duality, which is not really dual. I mean it should come to terms and exchange, and one should be able to imagine a kind of coupling, a strange coupling between enjoyment and war, or repression and acceptance, etc. One never goes without the other. We are Paradise losers. So, if you have an orange, then you'll have Iran, and vice versa: one gives or opens the door to the other. So I don't separate things. Is it something that must be endured? It's both – it all depends of course on how we feel – it's both painful and fruitful, it goes along together, always. What is important is not to forget: when you are in Hell not to forget Paradise and when you are in Paradise not to forget that it's going to end – that Paradise promises Hell, but that Hell promises Paradise.

And are you conscious of those two things in the writing?

Always. Always. That is, I'm not, for instance, very anxious when I write, because when I enjoy myself, which happens very often,

I don't start thinking it's going to end: I enjoy myself to the full and in the present. But I'm more aware of it, more dual, more dual conscious, when I suffer. Although when you suffer, you can only do but that – you suffer and you suffer and you suffer – there's also a little voice who reminds me, or knows, even if I can't remember, that suffering always has an end, even if it's by death.

I can be very upset with events. For instance, I get extremely upset when I read or when I hear about what happens in Israel and Palestine. I get the news directly all the time and I get extremely, extremely, extremely horrified and I despair. At the same time something in me is unaffected. It's a small place where there's a wisdom that knows it will have an end. Not everything is like that. I know that mourning, for instance, the loss of somebody dear to us, is in a way endless. Well, it finds new forms, it becomes less immediately aggressive, but it's endless.

The other is extremely important: without the other there cannot be writing. In the theatre, which you have called 'the immediate *site of the desire of the other' ('From the Scene of the Unconscious . . .' p. 12), you have worked on non Western European histories, voices and theatrical traditions: inflections of classical Noh theatre can be found in many of your theatrical works,* Tambours sur la digue *makes use of Japanese bunraku puppet theatre. Can you elaborate on how theatre is 'the* immediate *site of the desire of the other'?*

I shall do that shortly, because it deserves books and books since it's such a huge question. But first of all let me say that there's nothing without the other. This is so obvious it's a shame to have to say it. For instance, you kindly said that you had enjoyed my answers – there's the other coming out [*laughs*] – in the first part of our interview, but I didn't tell you that what I say is of course something which has gathered for years, it's a part of my experience of my thinking, but it does not emerge without the other. If you don't hold out your hand and your mind and your sympathy, to me: nothing exists. A large quantity of what *I* am supposed to *be*, or think, etc., is completely *provided* and *kindled* by the other. And for instance, if I have a dialogue with somebody who is completely closed, or blinded, or hostile, I myself become also – I am amputated of a part of myself. And it would be the same if I didn't pay attention to somebody: this person is reduced to nothing. It's simply the key to being human. Of course, the other is the god of creation, of presence. Now, when I say that the theatre is the *immediate* site of the other, it is ambiguous. It means, on one hand, that the theatre is the site of the desire that *I* have of the other, and on the other hand it means that it is the site of the desire that the other has of me. The genitive works two ways. Of course, theatre being the scene of the present *is* immediate – you *immediately* are with others, for others, thanks to others, in spite of others: they're there. It's the place where the individuality, the illusion one has and which is comparable to reality (now and then) that one can be alone, or separate, ends. Theatre is others. Always. In every way. When you write, when you perform, it's that. Now, your question then connects with the others as foreigners – since if you refer to non Western European histories, etc., it's because you extend the otherness to foreignness – and, of course, foreignness is simply the most spectacular incarnation of the other.

Why this insistence of 'non Western' voices, traditions, etc., in the theatre? That has to do with the specificity of theatre writing and in particular with that which is practised at the Théâtre du Soleil. The roots of theatre, the origins and the living practice of it, are situated in Asia, today, because Asia has preserved, has kept alive its most ancient traditions. When you go to Japan, or to Asia, you *are* in contact with the most archaic manifestations and phenomena, at the level of beliefs, at the level of art. You're in places, countries where the gods are *present*. You don't see that so much in Europe, in the West (except of course if you're a Catholic and if you believe that a certain person was a saint, etc.). This is something which is a minor aspect of Western culture. Western culture is without gods. But the gods *are* alive in their multiplicity and inventiveness in Asia. And the gods are, actually, the first characters in the theatre. Whether they are real gods (such as the hundreds of deities you have in India), or the other deities who are the characters of the unconscious (what the Greeks would call on when they used the words justice or oath – they made them into deities). So all the powers that we meet and that influence our lives, or which we have difficulties in coping with, etc., are *former* deities. This you see and these you meet, *actually*, if you go to Asia.

Which is why it's almost obvious that when you start on a theatrical way you are led to Asia. For instance, the Noh theatre has all the life of the Japanese *today* – although they are the most modern, developed people and culture they believe in ghosts. You know, they are related to ghosts, which the Africans are too. So ghosts, the dead are there are among you. If in the West you want to represent what is hidden behind the curtains of this belief, you just turn your eyes to these countries and there it is – there you have all the forms, the shapes, of haunting and possession of which we are the objects and subjects. Except that we tend to ignore, or interpret them differently. Now, as regards the puppet theatre: we are puppets. We don't always admit the fact and we imagine that we're autonomous or free, but it's not true: we're puppets. So it's quite natural that, in the only place which has survived the wiping out of former forces, which is the theatre, you'll find those shapes, those forms of expression. Noh always describes haunting. It's a haunting. All Noh plays tell of haunting. But we're haunted too, except that we don't express it as admirably, as poetically, as metaphorically.

And that immediacy of the other – I know for instance that when you're working on something for the theatre you are constantly working with the actors and with the director – is that part of it as well?

Oh yes, of course, of course. And it's a way of being reshaped, of bearing the marks of the others very, very quickly.

You memorably describe yourself in your 'Inter Views' with Mireille Calle-Gruber as 'a Talmudist of "reality"' (p. 56). Your Jewish heritage is becoming an increasingly important influence in your writing.

When I said that it was a metaphor. That is, it's the way the Talmudist would read the same little scene, or dialogue with a capacity for interpretation which is many, many fold. They will give you a hundred versions possible of this or that episode – which I think is admirable. There's no conclusive version, there are a hundred versions. And this is most important. Now, when I look at anything that happens in reality, any kind of event, I want a hundred versions of it. That's why I referred to that. But I won't avoid the question of my Jewish heritage. No, I don't think it's becoming *more* important. I think that – although it's very small and I haven't had a Jewish education, etc. – my secret memory, which is not even available for myself, is certainly impregnated with Jewish traces, but for me they belong to the poetical force which is at work in me and it has nothing to do of course with cult, or religion, or belief, but with a certain practice of reading which is *highly* developed in Jewish culture (when it exists, because it does not always exist). I think I am a mixture of forms of ancient cultures, because the Jewish heritage – to use a phrase, a ready-made phrase – is as present for me as the Greek one. I think that when I started reading the *Iliad* and the *Odyssey* all the situations and characters came to inhabit my imaginative world, leaving all kinds of traces, reflections on what mankind is, and it's simply mixed with what I harboured coming from the Biblical context. And for me it's the same thing, you know, there's a continuity. I can exchange or mix Ulysses and Samson, or David [*laughs*]. But it's a good thing – they can make a pair, which you can't do with Christianity, because it has ethical ambitions and pedagogical penchants, which the Bible doesn't have. The Bible doesn't teach you how to be good: it gives you only examples of evil [*laughs*]. And of failing. That's why I love it, because the greatest prophets – apart from Abraham, who is the only one who is sinless – all the prophets fail. All. All.

Your father, of course, has always been a presence in your writing, but it is only recently that you have written in depth about your mother. You make the comment in your short text 'In October 1991 . . .' that, although you have always written about your mother, it has been 'with extreme succinctness'; as you explain: 'It seems to me that we can't write about our mother. I'm sure about it. It's one of the limits of writing' (p. 47). This appears to be the close of the subject. And yet, when we reach Le jour où je n'étais pas là, *we find your mother's 'secrets', 'ses trésors les plus cachés et les plus dangereux [her most hidden her most perilous treasures]' (pp. 144–5), very beautifully, very fully, very lovingly described. Something extremely interesting happens in the interval between these two texts.*

Yes, well, I think I've come to terms with that . . . I thought it was
very funny, actually, the moment you proclaim in such an assured
way that you will never do such a thing, it means that you are on
the way to doing it . . . You know, when I said that, I wonder: what
was my state of mind? Did I believe myself? Certainly. Was I lying
to myself? No. I suppose that I was – what should I say, naïve?, it's
not even that – credulous enough to believe myself when I said
I was sure I'll never do it. It was probably a kind of unconscious
manipulation or manoeuvre to forbid myself from transgressing.
But you know, when you think in terms of transgression, you're on
the way to transgressing, you're already doing it. But at the same
time I was sincere, even though I was going round myself. I don't
know, maybe I could have obeyed the law, but it's impossible.
What triggered the reversal of the situation is something that happened when I wrote *Or, les lettres de mon père*. It all happened by a
kind of incredible accident (that is, the discovery of the letters of
my father which I didn't even know existed). Then it became for
me a dilemma, because I desperately wanted to write in the direction of my father again. And at the same time I desperately wanted
not to write, because I thought I'd written enough on my father.
It was terrible for me. And the result was *Or* . . . I mean, that was
the book. But it was not only that. I thought: *enough* of my father.
And I thought, at the same time, enough of my father means not
enough of my mother. So it gave way to the flood of my mother.
That's part of an explanation. The other part was the fact that my
mother in 1991 was 81: she was very young. And then later she was
85. And by and by I started to think the way she thought: time is
passing. It was a way of thinking I didn't want to accept. Then,
when she was 88, I couldn't resist, because she herself would also
say: you see I'm getting older. And behind this word there were so
many nostalgias and yearnings and the fear of separation. But not
only that, not only is my mother my mother, and much more
powerful and real than anything I can do in writing, not only did
I resist the idea of reducing her to a character in fiction, but there
was something else: that is the fact that my mother is a kind of
extraordinarily funny and wonderful casket, full of the treasures
of her own childhood, a whole world which has tragically disap-
peared – hundreds of people whom she remembers and of whom

she speaks about and for whom she's the only witness. And I thought it's true: all this world will disappear with her. It was an enormous world that was waving goodbye and I thought maybe I should not let them go like that. So, eventually I trespassed – that is, I thought what I shouldn't do I should do. And I started writing *Osnabrück*, that is the beginning, with the birthplace of my mother's memories, a city that has been emptied of its former Jewish community, etc. That's how it started. Not that I approved of myself. But I thought that I had to obey a law that maybe was more justified than the other law which forbids writing. So that's one thing. And when I had written *Osnabrück*, which was decided *by* the fact that it was my Osnabrück mother I wrote about, I thought: this is quite partial, it's ridiculous, this is only a small piece of the huge life and adventures of my mother, I haven't spoken of her as a midwife, I haven't spoken of her in Algeria and, you know, one thing just called for the other exactly as one word calls for the other. That's how it started. And after you have sinned once, as you know, you never stop [*laughs*]. So that's what happened.

Also in Le jour où je n'étais pas là *one finds the 'Choeur des Poules en Batterie [Chorus of Battery-Reared Chickens]' (pp. 103–5). Where did this hatch from?*

Battery-reared chickens are one of the things that can prevent me from sleeping. The ignominious way animals are treated and the industrialized way they are now treated, it's just a form of holocaust, I just can't bear it, just can't bear it. I think it's a crime, but it's one of the crimes for which there's no NGO – there's no NGO for the animals [in France]. And unfortunately most of the people who care for animals are, well, you know their discourse is not very well organized – in France they all belong to the extreme right, which is terrible. But for me there is no separation, no *strict* separation between animals and human beings and the way one allows human beings to suffer and the way one destroys them is of course non-admissible, but I feel my heart break when I think that those very same people who might be in sympathy with human victims would have no sympathy for animals. Whereas it's exactly the same type of cruelty which is evidenced by that. So, it makes me sick, it makes my love very tiring, because every time I think of it, or see pictures ... And I feel even more powerless regarding animals, because then the powers at work (that is, the food industries, the political powers), what can you do to stop them doing that? And, you know, sometimes I hear their advertisements on the radio which *seem* to be less inhuman and they ... These are farmers in France telling you that we who rear such-and-such chicken, we care for our chickens and for nature, we don't put them in batteries, they are free, they can have a happy life, which makes for the flesh to be the best you can taste – and it finishes like that. It's obvious they are right, they have to plead for nature-bred chicken, except that: they don't even realize that the message has a terrible ending. And when you're a child, you cry when you hear that. When you're a grown-up you eat. So this is not even analysed. At least analyse, at least know, at least hear – that's where the chorus comes from.

Do you still miss your myopia, what you call in Voiles/Veils *your 'secret non-seeing' (p. 16)?*

Yes, yes [*laughs*]. But sometimes I dream that I have it. Sometimes I dream as if time had not passed, that I'm looking desperately for my glasses [*laughs*]. And then I wake up and think but no ... I think that I don't want to be separate, from nothing do I want to be separate – I want to keep the evil, I want to keep the consciousness of the battery chickens, everything is part of me and I wouldn't like to forget or erase anything, really. So, yes. But of course I don't miss it in a unilateral way, that is I don't want to *be* short-sighted. I want to remember and besides, you know what, I realize that I am still short-sighted. First of all I'm short-sighted, because what I have discovered is that now I can see, which is a miracle, when you are short-sighted everything in your eye belongs to short-sightedness, so you can cut part of the cornea so that the lens is different, but the retina is that of a short-sighted person – you can't change that – so I'm *still* short-sighted, in a way.

Some of your early texts have recently appeared in new editions. Have you been rereading any of them?

Not really, no I haven't reread them. You know when they've been reprinted, I didn't reread them and probably I should have, because there were probably misprints, etc., but no.

Have you reread any of your former books?

It happens now and then that I do, although I don't like to do that, because some scholars ask me questions and if the question is very precise I have to go back and have a look at my book. But it's not something that I'm prone to do, really [*laughs*].

And what about your dream writing?[2]

This is different. The dreams are eternal, I can read them any time, it doesn't bother me, they are not works of art, they are productions of my unconscious, so it's OK. But with books it's different, because books carry with them something very temporal. They remind me of the time when I wrote them and who I was, etc. – and usually I don't like that. I prefer to forget [*laughs*].

Like looking at old photographs and seeing yourself in flared trousers . . .

Yes, I don't like that. I don't like photographs either. No. And it's strange because it's as if it's a kind of denial of myself, but it's probably that I must have a feeling that I'm not the one I was, I'm the one I shall be.

And when people talk about texts that you've written – which they do – ten, twenty years ago, how does that feel?

I can divide myself. That is, the part of me which is subjective does not want to relate. The part of me who teaches and who works on literature with scholars can accept it, scientifically. I might be interested, I might discuss, but it's outside of me. And then I feel that I respect the reading of others, I can try to answer, on the one hand as truthfully, on the other hand as systematically as possible. I feel responsible for that. And also there's something strange, you know, because it's as if there were incarnations of *me*. And I'm not sure if I want any kind of comparison, because they might be better than I am, or the reverse – I don't know [*laughs*].

And next? Do you plan your work in advance?

No. I don't plan ever. The only thing I plan is not planning. But I don't even plan that. I go to the birth of a book not knowing anything. I don't know its sex. I don't know what's it's going to be, whether it's a monster, whether it's going . . . Nothing at all. I just have a feeling, which is a very strange feeling, of trust. It's as if I believe that if I go to the place of appointment, it will come. That's all. I don't know who, I don't know how, I don't know what and through the years the only piece of knowing I have is that it will happen. That's all I know.

Chapter 7

Conclusion

> We do all this in order to follow, *not* to answer, the question, questions, which in French are feminine ... We *follow* the 'feminine' questions, asking: what is 'feminine' writing?
>
> (*Reading with C. L.*, p. 4)

Hélène Cixous's 'theory' of *écriture féminine*, 'feminine' writing, may indeed have started out as a response to, or defence against, a certain limiting, appropriating and destructive tendency in 'masculine' theoretical discourse, but over the years it has grown, flowered and spread to cover a wide, amorphous field of poetic writing, reading and thinking. In Cixous's early fictions, such as *Inside* and *The Third Body*, the 'I' takes centre stage. Her early writing engages in a quest of self-exploration, self-familiarization. It is a journey which the reader of her texts can only partially participate in. Although her 'theoretical' writing of this period stresses the need for writing to 'let go', to make room for the other, her fiction is several steps behind this ideal. Gradually, however, with texts such as *Angst*, *Vivre l'orange* and *Promethea*, other voices begin to make their presence felt. Cixous's writing passes through a time of change and rebirth. Following her discovery of the writing of Clarice Lispector, and her involvement in the work of Ariane Mnouchkine and the Théâtre du Soleil, her writing moves beyond 'the scene of the unconscious' and engages with the other in 'the scene of history'. *L'Indiade*, *Sihanouk* and *Manna* take her writing in new directions, into new genres. The process of creating these texts helps bring fresh impetus and focus to Cixous's overall writing project. Although her most recent writing re-engages with the personal (with her myopia, her memories of her childhood, her mother, and so on), it does so with a sense of ease, assurance and open-handedness. Cixous has found the means through which other voices, other selves, can enter into and inhabit (and cohabit) the many spaces of her writing. The 'I' is present, but it is an 'I' among others, with others, because of others. This same process of appearance-disappearance can be seen in the case of Cixous's 'theory' of *écriture féminine*. The radical experimentation and avant-garde polemics of her early 'theoretical' writing gradually gives way to more subtle, more effective approaches to the question of the 'feminine' (a word which is becoming increasingly synonymous with 'poetic'). Cixous's description of the approach taken to theory in the seminar at the Centre de Recherches en Etudes Féminines provides a good summary of the space *écriture féminine*, as 'theory', appears to occupy in her writing today:

> We are not outside theory in the seminar though I hope in a way we are above it. We use theoretical instruments, but we use them as aids, as a means of advancing further. This is not a way of repressing or obliterating theory but of giving it a place which is not an end in itself . . . We have all undergone our programme of theoretical initiation, but we have done this not to be confined by theory, but for theory to appear what it is, useful and traversable.
>
> ('Conversations', p. 144)

Useful and traversable. Cixous's view of *écriture féminine* is that it is a means to another end. It is something that she uses to get her writing going, something that she calls on to assist her in those times when she needs to ease her writing over or through some obstacle that has appeared in its way. The role played by 'theory' in Cixous's recent writing is that of the voice in the background, the prompter, the facilitator, the catalyst that enables the dialogic exchange between writing and the reader, writing and the other, to take place. In a sense, the less that one hears of 'theory' the better. If everything is running smoothly, there should be no reason to hear from it at all. As Cixous remarks, this is not to repress or to obliterate 'theory', it is simply to recognize it for what it is: useful and traversable. If there is a message that emerges from the development of Cixous's 'theory' of *écriture féminine*, 'a nugget of pure truth' that may be handed over to the reader (as Virginia Woolf once put it),[1] it is this: *write*. At its heart, Cixous's 'theory' is an encouragement to others to write and read for themselves, not to follow slavishly in her footsteps, but to set off on their own journeys, their own quests, to search out and explore their own questions. Speaking of the diaries of Etty Hillesum, a Jewish woman who was writing quite literally in the shadow of Auschwitz (Etty Hillesum died in Auschwitz on 30 November 1943), Cixous remarks: 'They can ... be read as a Bible of *savoir vivre*, of how to live and how to experience pleasure. My own recipe stays always the same. It consists in urging readers to plant flowers, both metaphorically and concretely' (*Readings*, p. 122).[2] Cixous's 'theory' presents the reader with examples of *savoir lire, savoir écrire* – how to read, how to write. Part of Cixous's intention with her 'theory' of *écriture féminine* is to offer a helping hand to get writing (and reading) going. Once this process has begun, her 'theory', useful and traversable, has arguably served its purpose. Cixous shows potential writers and readers various possible paths which they may or may not choose to take. Which path they do choose, and where they go from there, however, is a decision that she leaves entirely up to them.

Notes

Chapter 1: Introduction

1. 'Post-Word', trans. by Eric Prenowitz, in *Post-Theory: New Directions in Criticism*, ed. by Martin McQuillan, Graeme MacDonald, Robin Purves and Stephen Thompson (Edinburgh: Edinburgh University Press, 1999), pp. 209–13.
2. 'Le Rire de la Méduse', *L'Arc*, 61 (1975, 'Simone de Beauvoir et la lutte Des femmes'), 39–54.
3. 'The Laugh of the Medusa', trans. by Keith Cohen and Paula Cohen, *Signs*, 1:4 (Summer 1976), 875–93.
4. 'The Laugh of the Medusa', in *New French Feminisms*, ed. by Elaine Marks and Isabelle de Courtrivon (Amherst: University of Massachusetts Press, 1980), pp. 245–64.
5. 'The Laugh of the Medusa', in *The Signs Reader: Women, Gender, & Scholarship*, ed. by Elizabeth Able and Emily K. Able (Chicago: University of Chicago Press, 1983), pp. 279–97. All further references are to this edition.
6. Hélène Cixous and Catherine Clément, *La Jeune Née* (Paris: Union Générale d'Éditions, Collection 10/8, 1975), p. 6/back cover.
7. '*La Jeune Née*: an Excerpt', trans. by Meg Bortin, *Diacritics*, 7:2 (Summer 1977), 64–9.
8. 'Sorties: Where Is She . . .', trans. by Ann Liddle, in *New French Feminisms*, pp. 90–8.
9. 'Sorties: Out and Out: Attacks/Ways Out/Forays', in Hélène Cixous and Catherine Clément, *The Newly Born Woman*, trans. by Betsy Wing (Minneapolis: University of Minnesota Press, 1986), pp. 63–132. All references are to this edition.
10. 'We Are Already in the Jaws of the Book: Inter Views', in Hélène Cixous and Mireille Calle-Gruber, *Hélène Cixous Rootprints: Memory and Life Writing*, trans. by Eric Prenowitz (London: Routledge, 1997), pp. 1–115.

11. Cixous dislikes the term 'novel', referring to her texts in this genre as 'fictions' – a convention that is adopted throughout this book.

12. For a list of these translations (up until 1997), see the section entitled 'Non-French publications', in Marguerite Sandré and Eric Prenowitz, 'Hélène Cixous, Bibliography', in *Rootprints*, pp. 215–40 (pp. 229–40).

13. 'Albums and Legends', in *Rootprints*, pp. 177—206 (p. 198). Cixous is alluding to the oath given by Joyce's alter-ego, Stephen Dedalus, at the close of *A Portrait of the Artist as a Young Man*: 'So be it. Welcome, O life! I go to encounter for the millionth time the reality of experience and to forge in the smithy of my soul the uncreated conscience of my race ... Old father, old artificer, stand me now and ever in good stead.' James Joyce, *A Portrait of the Artist as a Young Man* (London: Jonathan Cape, 1956), p. 257.

14. 'My Algeriance, in other words: to depart not to arrive from Algeria', trans. by Eric Prenowitz, in *Stigmata: Escaping Texts* (London: Routledge, 1998), pp. 153–72 (p. 168).

15. Hélène Cixous and Ian Blyth, 'An Interview with Hélène Cixous', *Paragraph*, 23:3 (November 2000), 338–43 (pp. 338–9).

16. *Vivre l'orange/To Live the Orange*, trans. by Ann Liddle, Sarah Cornell and Hélène Cixous (Paris: Des femmes, 1979).

17. *L'Exil de James Joyce ou l'art du remplacement* (Paris: Publications de la Faculté des lettres et sciences de Paris-Sorbonne, 1969); repr. (Grasset, 1985); *The Exile of James Joyce*, trans. by Sally A. J. Purcell (New York: David Lewis, 1972); repr. (London: John Calder, 1976); repr. (New York: Riverrun, 1980).

18. As was explained above, all French nouns are either masculine or feminine. French adjectives have both masculine and feminine forms. In each case, an adjective takes its gender from the gender of the noun or pronoun it 'qualifies' or refers to. In general terms, the presence of a final '-e' at the end of an adjective is an indicator that it is the feminine form that is being used. For example: il est petit (he is small), elle est petite (she is small).

19. See, for example, 'My Algeriance'; and 'Stigmata, or Job the dog', trans. by Eric Prenowitz, in *Stigmata*, pp. 181–94.

20. 'Coming to Writing', trans. by Deborah Jenson, Ann Liddle and Susan Sellers, in *Coming to Writing and Other Essays*, ed. by Deborah Jenson (Cambridge, MA: Harvard University Press, 1991), pp. 1–58 (p. 17).

21. Mireille Calle-Gruber, 'Chronicle', in *Rootprints*, pp. 207–13 (p. 209).

22. *Dedans* (Paris: Grasset, 1969); *Inside*, trans. by Carol Barko (New York: Schocken, 1986). All references are to the English text.
23. 'From the Scene of the Unconscious to the Scene of History', trans. by Deborah W. Carpenter, in *The Future of Literary Theory*, ed. by Ralph Cohen (London: Routledge, 1989), pp. 1–18 (p. 4).
24. 'La Venue à l'écriture', in Hélène Cixous, Madeleine Gagnon and Annie Leclerc, *La Venue à l'écriture* (Paris: Union Générale d'Éditions, Collection 10/18, 1977), pp. 9–62; 'La Venue à l'écriture', in *Entre l'écriture* (Paris: Des femmes, 1986), pp. 6–69.
25. *Writing Differences: Readings from the Seminar of Hélène Cixous*, ed. by Susan Sellers (Milton Keynes: Open University Press/New York: St Martin's Press, 1988); *Reading with Clarice Lispector*, ed. and trans. by Verena Andermatt Conley (Minneapolis: University of Minnesota Press, 1990); *Readings: The Poetics of Blanchot, Joyce, Kafka, Kleist, Lispector, and Tsvetayeva*, ed. and trans. by Verena Andermatt Conley (Minneapolis: University of Minnesota Press, 1991).

Chapter 2: Feminine writing

1. An introduction, in English, to the work of Jacques Lacan can be found in *Écrits: A Selection*, trans. by Alan Sheridan (London: Tavistock, 1977). For Freud, see *The Standard Edition of the Complete Psychological Works of Sigmund Freud*, ed. and trans. by James Strachey and others, 24 vols (London: Hogarth Press/The Institute of Psycho-Analysis, 1953–74).
2. See Lacan, 'The Mirror Stage as Formative of the Function of the I as Revealed in Psychoanalytic Experience', in *Écrits*, pp. 1–7.
3. See Freud, 'Three Essays on the Theory of Sexuality', in *The Standard Edition of . . . Freud*, VII (1953), pp. 123–245 (esp. pp. 219–21).
4. See Freud, 'The Interpretation of Dreams', in *The Standard Edition of . . . Freud*, IV–V (1953).
5. 'Conversations', ed. and trans. by Susan Sellers, in *Writing Differences*, pp. 141–54 (pp. 144–5).
6. *Jouissance* refers to the whole spectrum of pleasure and enjoyment, sexual and otherwise. Since there is no single English word that is equivalent to this concept, *jouissance* is usually left untranslated. In fact, *jouissance* appears in the latest edition of the OED.
7. Virginia Woolf, *A Room of One's Own* and *Three Guineas*, ed. by Michèle Barrett (London: Penguin, 1993).
8. The slippage that occurs here from 'woman' to 'masculine' is significant – illustrating her own point about the dangers of 'anatomical'

determinants of sexual difference. Cixous is not comparing like with like. Nevertheless, the idea behind her point is made.

9. 'The Author in Truth', trans. by Deborah Jenson, Ann Liddle and Susan Sellers, in *Coming to Writing*, pp. 136–81 (p. 148). This is a revised version of a lecture originally given at the Paris International College of Philosophy in 1984. See 'Extreme Fidelity', trans. by Ann Liddle and Susan Sellers, in *Writing Differences*, pp. 9–36.

10. See Chapter 4 for a full discussion of Cixous's use of the term 'poetic'.

11. *The Gift: The Form and Reason for Exchange in Archaic Societies*, trans. by W. D. Halls (London: Routledge, 1990; repr. 1996), p. 39.

12. This point is emphasized in one of those accidents of language whereby the English verb 'to give birth' contains the sense of '*to give* birth' (an extra sense that is missing from the French verb '*accoucher*'). In English, then, one can say that 'birth' is something that one 'gives' to the other ('the gift of life' is another way of expressing this).

13. The image of children 'flying the nest' springs to mind here.

14. It must be noted that while her descriptions of the physical practice of *écriture féminine* have some aspects in common with the 'automatic writing' of the early Surrealists, Cixous's practice of writing is more rooted in thought, more deliberate, more connected to the conscious levels of being. There is also an uneasy undercurrent of patriarchal exploitation of women in early Surrealism (both in the imagery deployed and the 'role' of women in the movement). The practices of *écriture féminine* and automatic writing are very far from being the same thing.

Chapter 3: Fiction and theatre

1. See also 'The Character of "Character"', trans. by Keith Cohen, *New Literary History*, 5:2 (Winter 1974), 383–402.

2. *Le Troisième Corps* (Paris: Grasset, 1970); *The Third Body*, trans. by Keith Cohen (Evanston, IL: Northwestern University Press, 1999). Unless otherwise stated, all references are to the English text.

3. Roland Barthes, *S/Z*, trans. by Richard Miller (Oxford: Blackwell, 1990).

4. This play on words is reproduced in English equivalents by Cixous's translator: 'We acknowledge that things have been full of Zs theZe past few dayZ, as though the liZard had laid eggZ all over the place' (p. 115).

5. See, for example, the passage on p. 68, where Cixous alludes to Iago's comment to Roderigo, 'I am not what I am' (*Othello*, I. i. 65), and

then follows this with a quotation from Hamlet's exchange with the gravedigger: 'Am I where I am? "What man dost thou dig it for, my friend?" "For no man, sir" "What woman then?" "For none, neither"' (*Hamlet*, 5. i. 126–9).

6. Wilhelm Jensen, *Gradiva: ein pompejanisches Phantasiestück* (Dresden, 1903); Heinrich von Kleist, *The Marquise of O and Other Stories*, trans. by David Luke and Nigel Reeves (London: Penguin, 1978), pp. 51–67, 68–113.

7. Freud, 'Delusions and Dreams in Jensen's *Gradiva*', in *The Standard Edition of . . . Freud*, IX (1959), pp. 7–95.

8. A degree of caution must be exercised when speaking of 'the canon' in relation to a writer such as Cixous. As Cixous tells Alice Jardine and Anne M. Menke, she feels that it is an 'American' invention: 'this question of the twentieth-century canon does not exist here [in France]'. 'Hélène Cixous', trans. by Deborah Jenson and Leyla Roubi, in *Shifting Scenes: Interviews on Women, Writing and Politics in Post-68 France*, ed. by Alice Jardine and Anne M. Menke (New York: Columbia University Press, 1991), pp. 32–50 (p. 40).

9. *Les Commencements* (Paris: Grasset, 1970).

10. *Portrait du soleil* (Paris: Denoël, 1973).

11. *Portrait de Dora* (Paris: Des femmes, 1976); *Portrait of Dora*, trans. by Anita Barrows, *Gambit International Theatre Review*, 8:30 (1977), 27–67; *Portrait of Dora*, trans. by Sarah Burd, *Diacritics* (Spring 1983), 2–32.

12. Freud, 'Fragment of an Analysis of a Case of Hysteria', in *The Standard Edition of . . . Freud*, VII (1953), pp. 1–122.

13. *Un K. incompréhensible: Pierre Goldman* (Paris: Bourgois, 1975). Cixous's text is one of a number written at this time in support of Goldman, a Jewish political activist who, despite his protests of innocence, had been convicted of murder in 1974. The campaign in support of Goldman resulted in a retrial in 1976, at which Goldman was found innocent. However, he was later assassinated in 1979 by right-wing extremists. The details of his case, which also carry chilling echoes of the notorious 'Dreyfus' case of the late nineteenth, early twentieth century, have never been fully brought to light. Joseph K, Kafka's protagonist, like Goldman, is the victim of legal proceedings beyond his understanding or control. See Kafka, *The Trial*, trans. by Willa and Edwin Muir (London: Gollancz, 1935).

14. *Limonade tout était si infini* (Paris: Des femmes, 1982).

15. *Préparatifs de noces au-delà de l'abîme* (Paris: Des femmes, 1978); 'Wedding Preparations in the Country', trans. by Ernst Kaiser and

Eithne Wilkins, in *The Complete Short Stories of Franz Kafka*, ed. by Nahum N. Glatzer (London: Vintage, 1999), pp. 52–76.

16. *Partie* (Paris: Des femmes, 1976).

17. *Tombe* (Paris: Seuil, 1973), pp. 6–14.

18. *Neutre* (Paris: Grasset, 1972).

19. Poe's own epigraph (from Thomas Browne) to 'The Murders in the Rue Morgue', a passage from Baudelaire's translation of Poe, the same passage in English, and passages from the Swiss linguist Ferdinand de Saussure, the historian Heroditus, and Freud's *The Interpretation of Dreams*.

20. *Angst* (Paris: Des femmes, 1977); *Angst*, trans. by Jo Levy (London: John Calder/New York: Riverrun, 1985). Unless otherwise stated, all references are to the English text.

21. The main subject of 'The Author in Truth' is Clarice Lispector.

22. *Le Livre de Promethea* (Paris: Gallimard, 1983); *The Book of Promethea*, trans. by Betsy Wing (Lincoln, NE: University of Nebraska Press, 1991). All references are to the English text.

23. As both its French and English titles suggest: it might be 'about' Promethea, it might 'belong to' Promethea, it might even be 'by' Promethea.

24. This splitting of the narrative voice occurs in other texts by Cixous in this period. In Cixous's 1978 libretto, *Le Nom d'Oedipe: Chant du corps interdit* (*The Name of Oedipus: Song of the Forbidden Body*), the three 'solo' parts in the opera, Jocasta, Oedipus and Tiresias (there is also a chorus), are all doubled. By assigning Jocasta, Oedipus and Tiresias a 'singing' and a 'spoken' part the option is available for each 'role' to be played by two different people. In such an instance, both the singing and the speaking Jocastas, Oedipuses and Tiresiases would be on stage at the same time: providing visual, aural and thematic points of contrast and connection. This option was taken up at the opera's first performance – at the 1978 Festival d'Avignon, directed by Claude Régy. For an account of another, similar production of *The Name of Oedipus*, in 1991 at the Yale School of Drama, see Charlotte Canning, 'The Critic as Playwright: Performing Hélène Cixous' *Le Nom d'Oedipe*', *Lit: Literature Interpretation Theory*, 4:1 (1992, 'Hélène Cixous'), 43–55; repr. in *Hélène Cixous: Critical Impressions*, ed. by Lee A. Jacobus and Regina Barreca (Amsterdam: Gordon and Breach, 1999), pp. 305–25.

25. Philippe Lejeune, *On Autobiography*, ed. by Paul John Eakin, trans. by Katherine Leary (Minneapolis: University of Minnesota Press, 1989), p. 4.

26. Lejeune later rethought his position and, drawing on a phrase from one of Rimbaud's letters, conceded: 'If I have chosen the title *Je est un autre* in order to group the studies written since ['The Autobiographical Pact'], it is precisely to reintroduce the free play that is inevitably related to identity' (p. 125).

27. *La Pupille, Cahiers Renaud-Barrault*, 78 (Paris: Gallimard, 1972).

28. This is especially the case with the unperformed *La Pupille*, which features the Theatre among its cast of 'characters'.

29. *La Prise de l'école de Madhubaï, Avant-Scène du Théâtre*, 745 (March 1984), 6–22; repr. in *Hélène Cixous: Théâtre* (1986); *The Conquest of the School at Madhubaï*, trans. by Deborah Carpenter, *Women and Performance*, 3 (1986), 59–95. Phoolan Devi came from a poor, low-caste family. Having joined a band of violent bandits, she became famous in 1980 when 22 upper-caste men who had allegedly raped her were shot in 'revenge'. Denying that she was responsible for the killings, Devi eventually gave herself up to the police in 1982. After 11 years in jail (the case never went to trial) she was released in 1993 and went on to become a politician and a vocal campaigner for the rights of India's poor. Phoolan Devi was assassinated in 2001 by unknown gunmen.

30. *L'Histoire terrible mais inachevée de Norodom Sihanouk, roi du Cambodge* (Paris: Théâtre du Soleil, 1985; rev. 1987); *The Terrible but Unfinished Story of Norodom Sihanouk, King of Cambodia*, trans. by Juliet Flower MacCannell, Judith Pike and Lollie Groth (Lincoln, NE: University of Nebraska Press, 1994) [N.B. translation of original 1985 edition]; *L'Indiade, ou l'Inde de leurs rêves, et quelques écrits sur le théâtre* (Paris: Théâtre du Soleil, 1987).

31. 'A Realm of Characters', in *Delighting the Heart: A Notebook by Women Writers*, ed. by Susan Sellers (London: The Women's Press, 1989; repr. 1994), pp. 126–8.

32. *Richard III* (1981), *Twelfth Night* (1982) and *Henry IV* (1984). All three plays were translated by Mnouchkine. This was not the first time the company had performed Shakespeare. In 1968 the Théâtre du Soleil had put on a performance of *A Midsummer Night's Dream*, working with a translation by Philippe Léotard.

33. Cixous continues this practice in *Sihanouk*. For example, the role of the ghost of Norodom Suramarit, Sihanouk's father (who appears several times in the play), can be compared with the ghost of Hamlet's father.

34. For instance, in *Sihanouk* Madame Khieu Samnol, a vegetable merchant, and Madame Lamné, a Vietnamese fish merchant, are as

equally important to the plot as the king himself (or other historical figures, such as Saloth Sâr/Pol Pot and Henry Kissinger).

35. In *Sihanouk* (as Judith Pike points out in one of the introductions to the English translation), Sihanouk's passionate speech in Part 1, Act 1, Scene 1 – 'this other Eden, this demi-paradise, ... this happy breed of men, this little world, this blessed plot, ... this ANGKOR' (English text, pp. 37–8) – takes as its 'model' the 'scepter'd isle' speech by John of Gaunt in *Richard III* (see p. xvii).

36. Interestingly, *The Conquest of the School at Madhubaï* is in close conformity with the doctrine of the 'three unities', set down in Aristotle's *Poetics*, which declared that the action of a play should consist of a single plot (unity of action), in a single location (unity of place), with a time-span that is restricted to a single day (unity of time). Aristotle's doctrine of the three unities was hugely influential in seventeenth-century French theatrical writing (Corneille, Molière, etc.).

37. Politically and historically, the events described in both plays are still 'unfinished', unresolved.

38. The line between audience, actors and characters if often blurred. Norodom Sihanouk attended a performance of *Sihanouk* in Paris in 1985. Cixous has recently been working on a play about the refugees (or 'asylum seekers') who were interred in the now closed Sangatte detention centre near Calais. The actors in the play are all ex-inmates of Sangatte.

39. This passage also appears in another of Cixous's 'écrits sur le théâtre', 'L'Incarnation' ('Incarnation'), p. 265.

40. The closest either play comes to such a discussion is the prologue to part two of *Sihanouk* which, significantly, was not used in the actual performance (see pp. 107–9).

41. *Manne aux Mandelstams aux Mandelas* (Paris: Des femmes, 1988); *Manna for the Mandelstams for the Mandelas*, trans. by Catherine A. F. MacGillivray (Minneapolis: University of Minnesota Press, 1994). All references are to the English text.

42. Of the four persons mentioned in the title of the text, Winnie and Nelson Mandela perhaps require no introduction – although it is worth noting that *Manna* is published two years before Nelson Mandela's release from prison, at a time when the people of South Africa were still living under the system of racial/racist segregation known as apartheid. Nadezhda Mandelstam is best known today for her two powerful memoirs about life under Stalin: *Hope Against Hope: A Memoir*, trans. by Max Hayward (New York: Atheneum,

1970) and *Hope Abandoned*, trans. by Max Hayward (New York: Atheneum, 1974). Her husband, Osip Mandelstam, a poet and contemporary of Anna Akhmatova, Boris Pasternak and Marina Tsvetayeva, died in a Vladivostock labour camp in 1938.

43. Stalin was from Georgia, which neighboured on the Ossetic region. The last two lines of Mandelstam's poem read thus: 'Whatever the punishment he gives – raspberries, | and the broad chest of an Ossete'. See Osip Mandel'shtam, *Selected Poems*, trans. by David McDuff (Cambridge: Rivers Press, 1973), p. 131 (original Russian version, p. 130). The full text of the translation of Mandelstam's poem is also printed in the notes to *Manna* (pp. 265–6n).

44. Mandel'shtam, *Selected Poems*, pp. 150–9; *Manna*, pp. 287–90n.

45. *Jours de l'an* (Paris: Des femmes, 1990); *FirstDays of the Year*, trans. by Catherine A. F. MacGillivray (Minneapolis: University of Minnesota Press, 1998). All references are to the English text.

46. *L'Ange au secret* (Paris: Des femmes, 1991); *Déluge* (Paris: Des femmes, 1992).

47. Jardine and Menke, eds, *Shifting Scenes*, p. 33.

48. Cixous goes so far as to appear to give writing a name, 'Isaac' (see also *Déluge*); although, as Cixous tells Mireille Calle-Gruber, she is reluctant to explain why she has done so, preferring to allow the name 'to keep its mystery' (*Rootprints*, p. 92).

49. Clarice Lispector, *The Hour of the Star*, trans. by Giovanni Pontiero (Manchester: Carcanet, 1986; repr. 1992).

50. By which it is meant that the fiction contains and refers to many other texts. Strictly speaking, this is not the actual *intended* meaning of 'intertextuality', as defined by Julia Kristeva (who introduced the term in the 1960s). See Kristeva, 'Revolution in Poetic Language', in *The Kristeva Reader*, ed. by Toril Moi (Oxford: Blackwell, 1986; repr. 1996), pp. 89–136 (p. 111).

51. *Or, les lettres de mon père* (Paris: Des femmes, 1997).

52. *Beethoven à jamais ou l'existence de Dieu* (Paris: Des femmes, 1993).

53. *Les Euménides* (Paris: Théâtre du Soleil, 1992); *La Ville parjure ou le réveil des Erinyes* (Paris: Théâtre du Soleil, 1994).

54. *L'Histoire (qu'on ne connaîtra jamais)* (Paris: Des femmes, 1994). 'L'Histoire' can be translated as either 'The Story' or 'The History' – an ambiguity that Cixous deliberately plays upon.

55. *Tambours sur la digue: sous forme de pièce ancienne pour marionnettes jouée par des acteurs* (Paris: Théâtre du Soleil, 1999). See especially the essay by Cixous, 'Le Théâtre surpris par les marionnettes', that is printed at the back of the text (pp. 115–24).

56. *Voile Noire Voile Blanche/Black Sail White Sail*, trans. by Catherine A. F. MacGillivray, *New Literary History*, 25:2 (Spring 1994), 219–354.
57. The timeline of the play is given as: 'Between 1953 and 1960'; below this are printed the words: 'Stalin died on March 5, 1953' (p. 223).
58. *Osnabrück* (Paris: Des femmes, 1999).
59. *Le jour où je n'étais pas là* (Paris: Galilée, 2000); *The Day I Wasn't There*, trans. by Beverley Bie Brahic (forthcoming) – all translations from *Le Jour* are taken, with the kind permission of the translator, from a transcript of this translation; *Les Rêveries de la femme sauvage: scènes primitives* (Paris: Galilée, 2000). See also Chapter 6, where Cixous talks at length about the compulsion that has grown recently to bring her mother into her writing.
60. *Messie* (Paris: Des femmes, 1995); 'Shared at dawn', trans. by Keith Cohen, in *Stigmata*, pp. 175–80.
61. Cixous and Blyth, p. 342.

Chapter 4: Poetic theory

1. *Three Steps on the Ladder of Writing*, trans. by Sarah Cornell and Susan Sellers (New York: Columbia University Press, 1993). Derrida's words are quoted on the front and back cover.
2. 'The Last Painting or the Portrait of God', trans. by Sarah Cornell, Susan Sellers and Deborah Jenson, in *Coming to Writing*, pp. 104–31 (p. 124).
3. 'Writing blind: Conversation with the donkey', trans. by Eric Prenowitz, in *Stigmata*, pp. 139–52 (p. 144).
4. William Shakespeare, *The Sonnets* and *A Lover's Complaint*, ed. by John Kerrigan (London: Penguin, 1986).
5. For a more detailed account of Derrida's concept of *différance*, see the volume on Jacques Derrida in this series.
6. Contrary to the belief of a number of his Anglo-American critics, Derrida's concept of 'deconstruction' is more about opening up texts to the possibility of plurality and 'play', rather than taking them apart in a meaningless, nihilistic gesture. As Derrida explains: 'Here or there I have used the word *déconstruction*, which has nothing to do with destruction. That is to say, it is simply a question of ... being alert to the implications, to the historical sedimentation of the language we use.' Richard Macksey and Eugenio Donato, eds, *The Structuralist Controversy: The Languages of Criticism and the Sciences of Man* (Baltimore, MD: Johns Hopkins University Press, 1979), p. 271.

7. Hélène Cixous and Jacques Derrida, *Voiles* (Paris: Galilée, 1998); *Veils*, trans. by Geoffrey Bennington (Stanford, CA: Stanford University Press, 2001). All references are to the English text.

8. *Portrait de Jacques Derrida en Jeune Saint Juif* (Paris: Galilée, 2001).

9. Jacques Derrida, 'H. C. Pour la vie, c'est à dire', in *Hélène Cixous, croisées d'une oeuvre*, ed. by Mireille Calle-Gruber (Paris: Galilée, 2000), pp. 13–140.

10. Jacques Derrida, 'Circonfession', in Jacques Derrida and Geoffrey Bennington, *Jacques Derrida* (Paris: Seuil, 1991); 'Circumfession', in Jacques Derrida and Geoffrey Bennington, *Jacques Derrida*, trans. by Geoffrey Bennington (Chicago, IL: University of Chicago Press, 1993), pp. 3–315.

11. Eric Loret, 'Cixous déride Derrida', *Libération* (31 May 2001).

12. Like some of the textual experimentalism in Cixous's early fiction (see Chapter 3), the splashes of coloured text in *Portrait de Jacques Derrida* are reminiscent of the experiments in typography conducted by the early twentieth-century French poet Apollinaire. See Guillaume Apollinaire, *Calligrammes: Poèmes de la paix et la guerre (1913–1916)* (Paris: Gallimard, 1966).

13. The passage from 'Poem of the End' Cixous is commenting on is quoted in *Readings*, pp. 149–50. The full poem can be found in Marina Tsvetayeva, *Selected Poems*, trans. by Elaine Feinstein (New York: Dutton, 1987), pp. 48–72.

14. See also, Jacques Derrida, *Schibboleth. Pour Paul Celan* (Paris: Galilée, 1986).

15. Cixous and Blyth, 'An Interview with Hélène Cixous', p. 340.

16. 'Without end, no, State of drawingness, no, rather: The Executioner's taking off', trans. by Catherine A. F. MacGillivray, in *Stigmata*, pp. 20–31 (p. 20).

17. 'In October 1991 . . .', trans. by Keith Cohen, in *Stigmata*, pp. 35–49 (p. 35).

18. Cixous and Blyth, p. 340.

19. See *ibid.*, p. 339.

Chapter 5: Cixous on others: others on Cixous

1. *Le Prénom de Dieu* (Paris: Grasset, 1967).

2. Cixous and Blyth, 'An Interview with Hélène Cixous', pp. 338–9.

3. See Gérard Genette, *Paratexts: Thresholds of Interpretation*, trans. by Jane E. Lewin (Cambridge: Cambridge University Press, 1997), pp. 395–403.

4. Clarice Lispector, *Agua viva* (Artenova: Rio de Janeiro, 1973); *The Stream of Life*, trans. by Elizabeth Lowe and Earl Fitz (Minneapolis: University of Minnesota Press, 1989). All references are to the English translation. Cixous's 'Foreword' to the English translation (pp. ix–xxxv) is reprinted as part of the chapter on *The Stream of Life* in *Reading with Clarice Lispector* (pp. 15–24).

5. 1980–85, in the case of *Reading with Clarice Lispector*; 1982–84 for *Readings: The Poetics of Blanchot, Joyce, Kafka, Kleist, Lispector, and Tsvetayeva*.

6. 'Extreme Fidelity' (pp. 9–36) and 'Tancredi Continues' (pp. 37–53). 'Extreme Fidelity' is later revised and retranslated as 'The Author in Truth'.

7. Pierre Salesne, 'Hélène Cixous' *Ou l'art de l'innocence*: The Path to You' (pp. 113–26); Sarah Cornell, 'Hélène Cixous' *Le Livre de Promethea*: Paradise Refound' (pp. 127–40).

8. Gustave Flaubert, *Sentimental Education*, trans. by Robert Baldick (London: Penguin, 1974).

9. Clarice Lispector, ' Tanta mansidão', in *Onde estivestes de noite* (Artenova: Rio de Janeiro, 1974).

10. The following passage from an anonymous fifteenth-century English text, *The Cloud of Unknowing*, provides an interesting example of negative theology in practice, one that coincidentally illustrates Cixous's own thoughts on love, understanding and the other: 'But no man can think of God himself. Therefore, it is my wish to leave everything that I can think of and choose for my love the thing that I cannot think. Because he can certainly be loved, but not thought.' *The Cloud of Unknowing*, ed. by James Walsh, S. J. (London: SPCK, 1981), p. 130. Two of the key figures in the Christian tradition of negative theology are the fifth/sixth-century writer known as Pseudo-Dionysius and the late thirteenth-, early fourteenth-century German Dominican theologian, Meister Eckhart. Jacques Derrida has written extensively on negative theology and, in doing so, has sparked the creation of a whole sub-genre of commentary on his own comments. See, for example, Jacques Derrida, 'How to Avoid Speaking: Denials', trans. by Ken Frieden, in *Derrida and Negative Theology*, ed. by Harold Coward and Toby Foshay (Albany: State University of New York Press, 1992), pp. 73–142; and Luke Ferreter, 'How to avoid speaking of the other: Derrida, Dionysius and the problematic of negative theology', *Paragraph*, 24:1 (March 2001), 50–65.

11. A comprehensive list of works primarily, or significantly, concerned with the writing of Cixous can be found in the bibliography at the

end of this book. For more on Irigaray and Kristeva, see the volumes on these writers in this series.

12. Toril Moi, 'Hélène Cixous: An Imaginary Utopia', in *Sexual/ Textual Politics: Feminist Literary Theory* (London: Methuen, 1985), pp. 102–26 (p. 126).

13. Morag Shiach, *Hélène Cixous: A Politics of Writing* (London: Routledge, 1991).

14. Gayatri Chakravorty Spivak, 'French Feminism in an International Frame', *Yale French Studies*, 62 (1981), 154–84 (p. 175).

15. Verena Andermatt Conley, *Hélène Cixous: Writing the Feminine* (Lincoln, NE: University of Nebraska Press, 1984); see also Verena Andermatt Conley, *Hélène Cixous* (Toronto: University of Toronto Press/Hemel Hempstead: Harvester Wheatsheaf, 1992).

16. Susan Sellers, *Hélène Cixous: Authorship, Autobiography and Love* (Cambridge: Polity Press, 1996).

17. Julia Dobson, *Hélène Cixous and the Theatre: The Scene of Writing* (Bern: Peter Lang, 2002).

18. Gill Rye, *Reading for Change: Interactions Between Text and Identity in Contemporary French Women's Writing (Baroche, Cixous, Constant)* (Bern: Peter Lang, 2001).

19. For another excerpt (in English) from 'Fourmis', see Jacques Derrida, 'Foreword', trans. by Eric Prenowitz, in Susan Sellers, ed., *The Hélène Cixous Reader* (London and New York: Routledge, 1994), pp. vii–xiii. The full text of 'Fourmis' (in French) can be found in *Lectures de la Différence Sexuelle*, ed. by Mara Negron (Paris: Des femmes, 1994).

20. Only Derrida renders it *'la Cigale et le fourmi'* (p. 119).

21. Mireille Calle-Gruber, 'Hélène Cixous: Music Forever or Short Treatise on a Poetics for a Story To Be Sung', in *Hélène Cixous: Critical Impressions*, ed. by Jacobus and Barreca, pp. 75–90 (p. 80).

22. For example, a number of the papers given at a collquium held at Liverpool University in 1989, at which Cixous was the main speaker, can be found in *The Body and the Text: Hélène Cixous, Reading and Teaching*, ed. by Helen Wilcox, Keith McWatters, Ann Thompson and Linda R. Williams (Hemel Hempstead: Harvester Wheatsheaf, 1990). Cixous's contribution to this colloquium is the text 'Difficult Joys' (pp. 5–30). Readers of French can also consult the papers collected in *Hélène Cixous, chemins d'une écriture*, ed. by Françoise van Rossum-Guyon and Myriam Díaz-Diocaretz (Saint-Denis: Presses Universitaires de Vincennes/Amsterdam: Rodopi, 1990); and *Hélène Cixous, croisées d'une oeuvre*, ed. by Mireille Calle-Gruber

(Paris: Galilée, 2000). At the time of going to press, there are plans to publish the proceedings of a three-day colloquium hosted at the Bibliotéque Nationale de France on Cixous's work (*Genèses Généalogies Genres: Autour de l'oeuvre d'Hélène Cixous*, 22–24 May 2003), where the speakers included academics from a range of disciplines and countries, a psychoanalyst, critics, novelists, poets, theatre directors and actors.

Chapter 6: Cixous live

1. *Rouen, la Trentième Nuit de Mai '31* (Paris: Galilée, 2001).
2. Prior to this interview, we had been discussing Cixous's writing notebooks and looking at some of the dreams she had recorded in them.

Chapter 7: Conclusion

1. See Woolf, *A Room of One's Own*, p. 3.
2. Etty Hillesum, *An Interrupted Life: The Diaries and Letters of Etty Hillesum 1941–43* (London: Persephone, 1999).

Bibliography

Works by Hélène Cixous
Book-length publications in French

1967   *Le Prénom de Dieu* (Paris: Grasset)

1969   *Dedans* (Paris: Grasset) [Prix Médicis 1969] [repr. Des femmes, 1986]

——   *L'Exil de James Joyce ou l'art du remplacement* (Paris: Publications de la Faculté des lettres et sciences de Paris-Sorbonne) [repr. Grasset, 1985]

1970   *Les Commencements* (Paris: Grasset) [repr. Des femmes, 1999]

——   *Le Troisième Corps* (Paris: Grasset) [repr. Des femmes, 1999]

1971   *Un Vrai Jardin* (Paris: L'Herne) [repr. Des femmes, 1998]

1972   *Neutre* (Paris: Grasset) [repr. Des femmes, 1998]

——   *La Pupille, Cahiers Renaud-Barrault*, 78 (Paris: Gallimard)

1973   *Tombe* (Paris: Seuil)

——   *Portrait du soleil* (Paris: Denoël) [repr. Des femmes, 1999]

1974   *Prénoms de personne* (Paris: Seuil)

1975   and Catherine Clément, *La Jeune Née* (Paris: Union Générale d'Éditions, Collection 10/8)

——   *Un K. incompréhensible: Pierre Goldman* (Paris: Bourgois)

——   *Révolutions pour plus d'un Faust* (Paris: Seuil)

——   *Souffles* (Paris: Des femmes) [repr. 1998]

1976   *La* (Paris: Gallimard) [repr. Des femmes 1979]

——   *Partie* (Paris: Des femmes)

——   *Portrait de Dora* (Paris: Des femmes) [First performance 26 February 1976, Théâtre d'Orsay, dir. Simone Benmussa; version for radio broadcast 1972, Atelier de Création Radiophonique, France Culture] [repr. in *Hélène Cixous: Théâtre* (1986)]

1977   *Angst* (Paris: Des femmes) [repr. 1998]

—— with Madeleine Gagnon and Annie Leclerc, *La Venue à l'écriture* (Paris: Union Générale d'Éditions, Collection 10/18) [Title essay repr. in *Entre l'écriture* (1986)]

1978 *Le Nom d'Oedipe: Chant du corps interdit* (Paris: Des femmes) [Libretto, music composed by André Boucourechliev, first performance 1978, Festival d'Avignon, dir. Claude Régy]

—— *Préparatifs de noces au-delà de l'abîme* (Paris: Des femmes) [Excerpts read by Hélène Cixous, La Bibliothèque des voix, Des femmes (1981)]

1979 *Anankè* (Paris: Des femmes)

—— *Vivre l'orange/To Live the Orange* (Paris: Des femmes) [Bilingual] [repr. in *L'Heure de Clarice Lispector* (1989)]

1980 *Illa* (Paris: Des femmes)

1981 *(With) Ou l'art de l'innocence* (Paris: Des femmes)

1982 *Limonade tout était si infini* (Paris: Des femmes)

1983 *Le Livre de Promethea* (Paris: Gallimard)

1984 *La Prise de l'école de Madhubaï, Avant-Scène du Théâtre*, 745 (March), 6–22 [repr. in *Hélène Cixous: Théâtre* (1986)]

1985 *L'Histoire terrible mais inachevée de Norodom Sihanouk, roi du Cambodge* (Paris: Théâtre du Soleil) [First performance 11 September 1985, Théâtre du Soleil, dir. Ariane Mnouchkine] [Revised edition 1987]

1986 *La Bataille d'Arcachon* (Laval, Quebec: Trois)

—— *Entre l'écriture* (Paris: Des femmes)

—— *Hélène Cixous: Théâtre* (Paris: Des femmes) [*Portrait de Dora* and *La Prise de l'école de Madhubaï*]

1987 *L'Indiade, ou l'Inde de leurs rêves, et quelques écrits sur le théâtre* (Paris: Théâtre du Soleil) [First performance 30 September 1987, Théâtre du Soleil, dir. Ariane Mnouchkine]

1988 *Manne aux Mandelstams aux Mandelas* (Paris: Des femmes)

1989 and Ariane Mnouchkine, *La Nuit miraculeuse* (Paris: Théâtre du Soleil) [Television screenplay, broadcast December 1989, La Sept/FR3]

—— *L'Heure de Clarice Lispector, précédé de Vivre l'orange* (Paris: Des femmes)

1990 *Jours de l'an* (Paris: Des femmes)

1991 *L'Ange au secret* (Paris: Des femmes)

—— *On ne part pas, on ne revient pas* (Paris: Des femmes) [First reading 24 November 1991, (La Métaphore), dir. Daniel Mesguich and André Guittier]

1992 *Déluge* (Paris: Des femmes)

—— *Les Euménides* (Paris: Théâtre du Soleil) [First performance 26 May 1992, Théâtre du Soleil, dir. Ariane Mnouchkine] [Translation of Aeschylus, *The Furies*]

1993   *Beethoven à jamais ou l'existence de Dieu* (Paris: Des femmes)

1994   and Mireille Calle-Gruber, *Hélène Cixous: Photos de Racine* (Paris: Des femmes)

—— *L'Histoire (qu'on ne connaîtra jamais)* (Paris: Des femmes) [First performance 1994, Théâtre de la Ville/(La Métaphore), dir. Daniel Mesguich]

—— *La Ville parjure ou le réveil des Erinyes* (Paris: Théâtre du Soleil) [First performance 18 May 1994, Théâtre du Soleil, dir. Ariane Mnouchkine]

—— *Voile Noire Voile Blanche/Black Sail White Sail*, *New Literary History*, 25:2 (Spring), 219–354 [Bilingual]

1995   *La fiancée juive de la tentation* (Paris: Des femmes)

—— *Messie* (Paris: Des femmes)

1997   *Or, les lettres de mon père* (Paris: Des femmes)

1998   and Jacques Derrida, *Voiles* (Paris: Galilée)

1999   *Portrait de l'artiste en personnage de roman: roman* (Paris: Hartmann)

—— *Osnabrück* (Paris: Des femmes)

—— *Tambours sur la digue: sous forme de pièce ancienne pour marionnettes jouée par des acteurs* (Paris: Théâtre du Soleil) [First performance November 1999, Théâtre du Soleil, dir. Ariane Mnouchkine]

2000   *Le jour où je n'étais pas là* (Paris: Galilée)

—— *Les Rêveries de la femme sauvage: scènes primitives* (Paris: Galilée)

2001   *Benjamin à Montaigne: il ne faut pas le dire* (Paris: Galilée)

—— *Portrait de Jacques Derrida en Jeune Saint Juif* (Paris: Galilée)

—— *Rouen, la Trentième Nuit de Mai '31* (Paris: Galilée) [First reading 1998, colloque de Cerisy ('Hélène Cixous: Croisées d'une oeuvre'), dir. Daniel Mesguich and Luce Mouchel; first performance, with music by Jean-Jacques Lemêtre, 18 July 2001, Villeneuve-lès-Avignon, dir. Daniel Mesguich]

2002   *Manhattan: Lettres de la préhistoire* (Paris: Galilée)

2003   *L'amour du loup et autres remords* (Paris: Galilée)

—— *Rêve je te dis* (Paris: Galilée)

Book-length publications in English

1972   *The Exile of James Joyce*, trans. by Sally A. J. Purcell (New York: David Lewis) [repr. (London: John Calder, 1976); repr. (New

York: Riverrun, 1980)] [Translation of *L'Exil de James Joyce ou l'art du remplacement* (1969)]

1977   *Portrait of Dora*, trans. by Anita Barrows, *Gambit International Theatre Review*, 8:30, 27–67 [repr. in *Benmussa Directs* (London: John Calder/Dallas: Riverrun, 1979)] [Translation of *Portrait de Dora* (1976)]

1979   *Vivre l'orange/To Live the Orange*, trans. by Ann Liddle, Sarah Cornell and Hélène Cixous (Paris: Des femmes) [Bilingual]

1983   *Portrait of Dora*, trans. by Sarah Burd, *Diacritics* (Spring), 2–32 [Translation of *Portrait de Dora* (1976)]

1985   *Angst*, trans. by Jo Levy (London: John Calder/New York: Riverrun) [Translation of *Angst* (1977)]

1986   *The Conquest of the School at Madhubaï*, trans. by Deborah Carpenter, *Women and Performance*, 3, 59–95 [Translation of *La Prise de l'école de Madhubaï* (1984)]

——   *Inside*, trans. by Carol Barko (New York: Schocken) [Translation of *Dedans* (1969)]

——   and Catherine Clément, *The Newly Born Woman*, trans. by Betsy Wing (Minneapolis: University of Minnesota Press) [Translation of *La Jeune Née* (1975)]

1988   'Neutre', trans. by Lorene M. Birden, in 'Making English Clairielle: An Introduction and Translation for Hélène Cixous' "Neutre"' (Unpublished MA Thesis, University of Massachusetts at Amherst) [Translation of *Neutre* (1972)]

1990   *Reading with Clarice Lispector*, ed. and trans. by Verena Andermatt Conley (Minneapolis: University of Minnesota Press) [Abridged transcripts of seminars at the Centre de Recherches en Etudes Féminines, 1980–85]

1991   *The Book of Promethea*, trans. by Betsy Wing (Lincoln, NE: University of Nebraska Press) [Translation of *Le Livre de Promethea* (1983)]

——   *Coming to Writing and Other Essays*, ed. by Deborah Jenson, trans. by Sarah Cornell, Deborah Jenson, Ann Liddle and Susan Sellers (Cambridge, MA: Harvard University Press) [Translation of selections from *La Venue à l'écriture* (1977), *Entre l'écriture* (1986) and *L'Heure de Clarice Lispector* (1989)]

——   *Readings: The Poetics of Blanchot, Joyce, Kafka, Kleist, Lispector, and Tsvetayeva*, ed. and trans. by Verena Andermatt Conley (Minneapolis: University of Minnesota Press) [Abridged transcripts of seminars at the Centre de Recherches en Etudes Féminines, 1982–84]

1993   *Three Steps on the Ladder of Writing*, trans. by Sarah Cornell
and Susan Sellers (New York: Columbia University Press)
[The Wellek Library Lectures in Critical Theory, Irvine, CA,
1990]

1994   *The Hélène Cixous Reader*, ed. by Susan Sellers, trans. by Susan
Sellers and others (London: Routledge) [repr. 1996] [Includes
translated excerpts from *Dedans* (1969), *Neutre* (1972), *Prénoms de
personne* (1974), *La Jeune Née* (1975), *Souffles* (1975), *La* (1976),
Angst (1977), *Vivre l'orange/To Live the Orange* (1979), *(With) Ou
l'art de l'innocence* (1981), *Limonade tout était si infini* (1982), *Le
Livre de Promethea* (1983), 'Extreme Fidelity' (1988), *L'Histoire
terrible mais inachevée de Norodom Sihanouk, roi du Cambodge* (1985),
L'Indiade, ou l'Inde de leurs rêves (1987), *Manne aux Mandelstams aux
Mandelas* (1988), *Jours de l'an* (1990), *Déluge* (1992) and *Three
Steps on the Ladder of Writing* (1993)]

——   *Manna for the Mandelstams for the Mandelas*, trans. by Catherine
A. F. MacGillivray (Minneapolis: University of Minnesota Press)
[Translation of *Manne aux Mandelstams aux Mandelas* (1988)]

——   *The Name of Oedipus: Song of the Forbidden Body*, trans. by Christiane Makward, in *Plays by French and Francophone Women: A Critical Anthology*, ed. by Christiane Makward and Judith G. Miller
(Ann Arbor: University of Michigan Press) [Translation of *Le
Nom d'Oedipe* (1978)]

——   *The Terrible but Unfinished Story of Norodom Sihanouk, King of Cambodia*, trans. by Juliet Flower MacCannell, Judith Pike and Lollie
Groth (Lincoln, NE: University of Nebraska Press) [Translation
of *L'Histoire terrible mais inachevée de Norodom Sihanouk, roi du Cambodge* (1985); N.B. translation of original edition]

——   *Voile Noir Voile Blanche/Black Sail White Sail*, trans. by Catherine
A. F. MacGillivray, *New Literary History*, 25:2 (Spring), 219–354
[Bilingual]

1996   with Marilyn French and Mario Vargas Llosa, *Bloom* (Dublin:
Kingstown Press)

1997   and Mireille Calle-Gruber, *Hélène Cixous Rootprints: Memory and
Life Writing*, trans. by Eric Prenowitz (London: Routledge)
[Translation of *Hélène Cixous: Photos de Racine* (1994)]

1998   *FirstDays of the Year*, trans. by Catherine A. F. MacGillivray
(Minneapolis: University of Minnesota Press) [Translation of
Jours de l'an (1990)]

——   *Stigmata: Escaping Texts*, trans. by Keith Cohen, Catherine A. F.
MacGillivray and Eric Prenowitz (London: Routledge)

1999   *The Third Body*, trans. by Keith Cohen (Evanston, IL: Northwestern University Press) [Translation of *Le Troisième Corps* (1970)]

2000   *A True Garden*, trans. by Claudine G. Fisher, *Paragraph*, 23:3 (November), 252–7 [Translation of *Un Vrai Jardin* (1971)]

2001   and Jacques Derrida, *Veils*, trans. by Geoffrey Bennington (Stanford, CA: Stanford University Press) [Translation of *Voiles* (1998)]

2003   *The Plays of Hélène Cixous*, trans. by Bernadette Fort, Donald Watson, Ann Liddle, Judith G. Miller and Brian J. Mallet (London: Routledge) [Translations of *La Ville parjure ou le réveil des Erinyes* (1994); *Voile Noire Voile Blanche* (1994); *Portrait de Dora* (1976); *Tambours sur la digue* (1999)]

2004   *Writing Notebooks*, ed. and trans. by Susan Sellers (London: Continuum)

——   *Portrait of Jacques Derrida as a Young Jewish Saint*, trans. by Beverley Bie Brahic (New York: Columbia University Press) [Translation of *Portrait de Jacques Derrida en Jeune Saint Juif* (2001)]

——   *Reveries of the Wild Woman: Primal Scenes*, trans. by Brian Mallet (Evanston, IL: Northwestern University Press) [Translation of *Les Rêveries de la femme sauvage: scènes primitives* (2000)]

(forthcoming)   *The Day I Wasn't There*, trans. by Beverley Bie Brahic [Translation of *Le jour où je n'étais pas là* (2000)]

Articles in English

1974   'The Character of "Character"', trans. by Keith Cohen, *New Literary History*, 5:2 (Winter), 383–402

——   'Political Ignominy: "Ivy Day"', in *Joyce: A Collection of Critical Essays* ('Twentieth-Century Views'), ed. by William M. Chace (Englewood Cliffs, NJ: Prentice Hall), pp. 11–17

1975   'At Circe's, or the Self-Opener', trans. by Carol Bové, *Boundary 2*, 3:2 (Winter), 387–97 [repr. in *Early Postmodernism, Foundational Essays*, ed. by Paul Bové (Durham, NC: Duke University Press, 1995), pp. 175–87]

1976   'Fiction and its Phantoms: A Reading of Freud's *Das Unheimlich* ("The Uncanny")', trans. by R. Dennommé, *New Literary History*, 7:3 (Spring), 525–48

——   'The Fruits of Femininity', *Guardian* (Manchester) (16 May), 10

——   'The Laugh of the Medusa', trans. by Keith Cohen and Paula Cohen, *Signs*, 1:4 (Summer), 875–93 [repr. in *New French Feminisms*, ed. by Elaine Marks and Isabelle de Courtrivon (Amherst:

University of Massachusetts Press, 1980); repr. (Brighton: Harvester/New York: Schocken, 1981), pp. 245–64; repr. in *The Signs Reader: Women, Gender, & Scholarship*, ed. by Elizabeth Able and Emily K. Able (Chicago: University of Chicago Press, 1983), pp. 279–97; repr. in *Critical Theory Since 1965*, ed. by Hazard Adams and Leroy Searle (Tallahassee: University Presses of Florida/Florida State University Press, 1986), pp. 309–20]

1977   '*La Jeune Née*: an Excerpt', trans. by Meg Bortin, *Diacritics*, 7:2 (Summer), 64–9

——   'Boxes', trans. by Rosette C. Lamont, *Centrepoint* (City University of New York), 2:3 [7] (Autumn), 30–1

——   '*Partie*: an Extract', trans. by Keith Cohen, *TriQuarterly*, 38 (Winter), 95–100

1980   'Arrive le chapitre-qui-vient (Come the Following Chapter)', trans. by Stan Theis, *Enclitic*, 4:2 (Autumn), 45–58

——   'Sorties: Where Is She . . .', trans. by Ann Liddle, in *New French Feminisms*, ed. by Elaine Marks and Isabelle de Courtivron (Amherst: University of Massachusetts Press), pp. 90–8 [repr. (Brighton: Harvester/New York: Schocken, 1981)]

——   'Poetry is/and (the) Political', trans. by Ann Liddle, *Bread and Roses*, 2:1, 16–18

1981   'Castration or Decapitation?', trans. by Annette Kuhn, *Signs*, 7:1 (Autumn), 41–55 [repr. in *Contemporary Literary Criticism: Literary and Cultural Studies*, ed. by Robert Con Davis and Ronald Schleifer, 2nd edn (New York: Longman, 1989), pp. 479–91; repr. in *Authorship: From Plato to the Postmodern, A Reader*, ed. by Seán Burke (Edinburgh: Edinburgh University Press, 1995), pp. 162–77]

1982   'Comment on Women's Studies in France', *Signs*, 7:3 (Spring), 721–2

——   'The Step', trans. by Jill McDonald and Carole Deering Paul, *The French-American Review*, 6:1 (Spring), 27–30

——   'Introduction to Lewis Carroll: *Through the Looking Glass* and *The Hunting of the Snark*', trans. by Marie Maclean, *New Literary History*, 13:2 (Winter), 231–51

1984   'Going to the Seashore', trans. by Barbara Kerstlake, *Modern Drama*, 27:4 (December), 546–8

——   'Joyce: the (R)use of Writing', trans. by Judith Still, in *Post-Structuralist Joyce: Essays from the French*, ed. by Derek Attridge and Daniel Ferrer (Cambridge: Cambridge University Press), pp. 15–30

—— '12 août 1980. August 12, 1980', trans. by Betsy Wing, *Boundary 2*, 12:2 (Winter), 8–39 [Bilingual]

—— 'Reading Clarice Lispector's "Sunday before going to sleep"', trans. by Betsy Wing, *Boundary 2*, 12:2 (Winter), 41–8

1985 'The Meadow', trans. by Penny Hueston and Christina Thompson, *Scripsi*, 3:4 ('Special French Issue'), 101–12

1986 'The Last Word', trans. by Ann Liddle and Susan Sellers, *The Women's Review*, 6 (April), 22–4 [Translation of excerpt from *Le Livre de Promethea* (1983)]

—— 'The Language of Reality', in *Twentieth Century British Literature 3: James Joyce:* Ulysses, ed. by Harold Bloom (New York: Chelsea House), pp. 1502–5

1987 'Her Presence Through Writing', trans. by Deborah Carpenter, *Literary Review*, 30 (Spring), 445–53 [See 'Coming to Writing' (1991)]

—— '*The Book of Promethea*: Five Excerpts', trans. by Deborah Carpenter, *Frank*, 6:7 (Winter–Spring), 42–4

—— 'Reaching the Point of Wheat, or A Portrait of the Artist as a Maturing Woman', *New Literary History*, 19:1, 1–21

—— 'The Parting of the Cake', trans. by Franklin Philip, in *For Nelson Mandela*, ed. by Jacques Derrida and Mustapha Tlili (New York: Seaver Books), pp. 201–18

—— 'Life Without Him Was Life Without Him', *New York Times Book Review*, 7 (1 November), 35 [Excerpt from 'The Parting of the Cake' (1987)]

1988 'Extreme Fidelity', trans. by Ann Liddle and Susan Sellers, in *Writing Differences: Readings from the Seminar of Hélène Cixous*, ed. by Susan Sellers (Milton Keynes: Open University Press/ New York: St Martin's Press), pp. 9–36 [see 'The Author in Truth' (1991)]

—— 'Tancredi Continues', trans. by Ann Liddle and Susan Sellers, in *Writing Differences: Readings from the Seminar of Hélène Cixous*, ed. by Susan Sellers (Milton Keynes: Open University Press/New York: St Martin's Press), pp. 37–53 [revised translation in *Coming to Writing and Other Essays* (1991), pp. 152–68]

1989 'Foreword', trans. by Verena Andermatt Conley, in Clarice Lispector, *The Stream of Life*, trans. by Elizabeth Lowe and Earl Fitz (Minneapolis: University of Minnesota Press) [See *Reading with Clarice Lispector* (1990), pp. 15–24]

—— 'Writings on the Theater', trans. by Catherine Franke, *Qui Parle* (University of California, Berkeley), 3:1 (Spring), 120–35

[Translation of excerpts from *L'Indiade, ou l'Inde de leurs rêves* (1987); see 'The Place of Crime, The Place of Forgiveness' (1994)]

——— 'Dedication to the Ostrich', trans. by Catherine Franke, *Qui Parle* (University of California, Berkeley), 3:1 (Spring), 135–52

——— 'From the Scene of the Unconscious to the Scene of History', trans. by Deborah W. Carpenter, in *The Future of Literary Theory*, ed. by Ralph Cohen (London: Routledge), pp. 1–18

1990 'Difficult Joys', in *The Body and the Text: Hélène Cixous, Reading and Teaching*, ed. by Helen Wilcox, Keith McWatters, Ann Thompson and Linda R. Williams (Hemel Hempstead: Harvester Wheatsheaf), pp. 5–30

——— Excerpt from *Vivre l'orange/To Live the Orange*, in *The Virago Book of Poetry* (London: Virago), pp. 210–11

1991 'Coming to Writing', trans. by Deborah Jenson, Ann Liddle and Susan Sellers, in *Coming to Writing and Other Essays*, pp. 1–58

——— 'Clarice Lispector: The Approach. Letting Oneself (be) Read (by) Clarice Lispector. The Passion According to C. L.', trans. by Sarah Cornell, Susan Sellers and Deborah Jenson, in *Coming to Writing and Other Essays*, pp. 59–77

——— 'The Last Painting or the Portrait of God', trans. by Sarah Cornell, Susan Sellers and Deborah Jenson, in *Coming to Writing and Other Essays*, pp. 104–31

——— 'By the Light of an Apple', trans. by Deborah Jenson, in *Coming to Writing and Other Essays*, pp. 132–5

——— 'The Author in Truth', trans. by Deborah Jenson, Ann Liddle and Susan Sellers, in *Coming to Writing and Other Essays*, pp. 136–81

1992 'The Day of Condemnation', trans. by Catherine A. F. MacGillivray, *LIT: Literature Interpretation Theory*, 4:1 ('Hélène Cixous'), 1–16

1993 'Bathsheba or the interior Bible', trans. by Catherine A. F. MacGillivray, *New Literary History*, 24:4, 820–37 [repr. in *Stigmata: Escaping Texts* (1998), pp. 3–19]

——— 'We who are free, are we free?', trans. by Chris Miller, *Critical Inquiry*, 19:2, 201–19 [repr. in *Freedom and Interpretation*, ed. by Barbara Johnson (New York: Basic Books), pp. 17–44]

——— 'Without end, no, State of drawingness, no, rather: The Executioner's taking off', trans. by Catherine A. F. MacGillivray, *New Literary History*, 24:1 (Winter), 90–103 [repr. in *Stigmata: Escaping Texts* (1998), pp. 20–31]

1994   'The Coup', and 'It is the Story of a Star', trans. by Stéphanie
       Lhomme and Helen Carr, *Women: a cultural review*, 5:2, 113–22
──   'Preface', trans. by Susan Sellers, in *The Hélène Cixous Reader*,
       pp. xv–xxiii
──   'The Place of Crime, The Place of Forgiveness', trans. by Cath-
       erine A. F. MacGillivray, in *The Hélène Cixous Reader*, pp. 150–6
       [Revised translation of an excerpt from 'Writings on the Thea-
       ter' (1989)]
1995   'Great Tragic Characters ...', *The Times Literary Supplement*
       (28 April), 15
1996   'Attacks of the Castle', trans. by Eric Prenowitz, in *Beyond the
       Wall: Architecture, Ideology and Culture in Central and Eastern Europe*,
       ed. by Neil Leach (London: Routledge), 302–7 [repr. in *Architec-
       ture and Revolution*, ed. by Neil Leach (London: Routledge, 1999),
       pp. 228–33]
──   'An Error of Calculation', trans. by Eric Prenowitz, *Yale French
       Studies*, 89, 151–4
──   ' "Mamãe, disse ele", or Joyce's Second Hand', trans. by Eric Pre-
       nowitz, *Poetics Today*, 17:3 (Autumn), 339–66 [repr. in *Stigmata:
       Escaping Texts* (1998), pp. 100–128; repr. in *Exile and Creativity:
       Signposts, Travelers, Outsiders, Backward Glances*, ed. by Susan
       Rubin Suleiman (Durham, NC: Duke University Press, 1998),
       pp. 59–88]
──   'In October 1991 ...', trans. by Catherine McGann, in *On the
       Feminine*, ed. by Mireille Calle-Gruber (New Jersey: Humanities
       Press), pp. 77–92 [see 'In October 1991 ...' (1998)]
──   'Writing Blind', trans. by Eric Prenowitz, *TriQuarterly*, 97
       (Autumn), 7–20 [revised translation by Eric Prenowitz, 'Writing
       blind: Conversation with the donkey', in *Stigmata: Escaping Texts*
       (1998), pp. 139–52]
1997   'My Algeriance, in other words: to depart not to arrive from
       Algeria', trans. by Eric Prenowitz, *TriQuarterly*, 100, 259–79
       [repr. in *Stigmata: Escaping Texts* (1998), pp. 153–72]
──   'Stigmata, or Job the dog', trans. by Eric Prenowitz, *Philosophy
       Today*, 41:1 (Spring), 12–17 [repr. in *Stigmata: Escaping Texts*
       (1998), pp. 181–94]
──   'Quelle heure est-il?', in *Hélène Cixous Rootprints: Memory and Life
       Writing*, pp. 128–33
──   'Albums and Legends', in *Hélène Cixous Rootprints: Memory and Life
       Writing*, pp. 177–206

1998   'Letter to Zohra Drif', trans. by Eric Prenowitz, *Parallax*, 4:2 (April–June), 189–96

——   'In October 1991 . . .', trans. by Keith Cohen, in *Stigmata: Escaping Texts*, pp. 35–49 [see 'In October 1991 . . .' (1996)]

——   'Hiss of the Axe', trans. by Keith Cohen, in *Stigmata: Escaping Texts*, pp. 50–6

——   'What is it o'clock? or The door (we never enter)', trans. by Catherine A. F. MacGillivray, in *Stigmata: Escaping Texts*, pp. 57–83

——   'Love of the Wolf', trans. by Keith Cohen, in *Stigmata: Escaping Texts*, pp. 84–99

——   'Unmasked!', trans. by Keith Cohen, in *Stigmata: Escaping Texts*, pp. 131–8

——   'Shared at dawn', trans. by Keith Cohen, in *Stigmata: Escaping Texts*, pp. 175–80

1999   'Enter the Theater (in Between)', trans. by Brian J. Mallet, *Modern Drama*, 42:3 (Autumn), 301–14

——   'Hélène Cixous, OR: My Father's Letters', trans. by Kim Allen, Adele Parker and Stephanie Young, *Beacons*, 5, 121–6

——   'Post-Word', trans. by Eric Prenowitz, in *Post-Theory: New Directions in Criticism*, ed. by Martin McQuillan, Graeme MacDonald, Robin Purves and Stephen Thompson (Edinburgh: Edinburgh University Press), pp. 209–13

2001   'With a blow of the wand', *Parallax*, 7:2 (April–June), 85–94

Interviews in English

1976   (with Christiane Makward), 'Interview', trans. by Ann Liddle and Beatrice Cameron, *Substance*, 13, 19–37

——   'The Fruits of Femininity', *Manchester Guardian Weekly* (16 May), 14

1979   'Rethinking Differences: An Interview', trans. by Isabelle de Courtivron, in *Homosexualities and French Literature*, ed. by Elaine Marks and Georges Stambolian (Ithaca: Cornell University Press), pp. 70–88 [Interview from 1976]

1984   (with Verena Andermatt Conley), 'An Exchange with Hélène Cixous', in Verena Andermatt Conley, *Hélène Cixous: Writing the Feminine* (Lincoln, NE: University of Nebraska Press), pp. 129–61

1985   (with Susan Sellers), 'Hélène Cixous', *The Women's Review* (7 May), 22–3

1987   (with Linda Brandon), 'Impassive resistance', *Independent* (11 November)

1988 (with members of the Centre d'Etudes Féminines), 'Conversations', ed. and trans. by Susan Sellers, in *Writing Differences: Readings from the Seminar of Hélène Cixous*, ed. by Susan Sellers (Milton Keynes: Open University Press/New York: St Martin's Press), pp. 141–54

—— (with Alice Jardine and Anne M. Menke), 'Exploding the Issue: "French" "Women" "Writers" and "The Canon"', trans. by Deborah Carpenter, *Yale French Studies*, 75, 235–6

1989 (with Susan Sellers), 'The Double World of Writing', 'Listening to the Heart', 'A Realm of Characters', 'Writing as a Second Heart', in *Delighting the Heart: A Notebook by Women Writers*, ed. by Susan Sellers (London: The Women's Press; repr. 1994), pp. 18, 69, 126–8, 198

—— (with Catherine Franke and Roger Chazal), 'Interview with Hélène Cixous', *Qui Parle* (University of California, Berkeley), 3:1 (Spring), 152–79

1991 (with Alice Jardine and Anne M. Menke), 'Hélène Cixous', trans. by Deborah Jenson and Leyla Roubi, in *Shifting Scenes: Interviews on Women, Writing and Politics in Post-68 France*, ed. by Alice Jardine and Anne M. Menke (New York: Columbia University Press), pp. 32–50

1997 (with Bernadette Fort Greenblatt), 'Theater, History, Ethics: An Interview with Hélène Cixous on the Perjured City, or the Awakening of the Furies', *New Literary History*, 28:3, 425–56

—— (with Mireille Calle-Gruber), 'We Are Already in the Jaws of the Book: Inter Views', in *Hélène Cixous Rootprints: Memory and Life Writing*, pp. 1–115

2000 'Hélène Cixous in Conversation with Sophia Phoca', *Wasafiri* (London), 31 (Spring), 9–13

—— (with Ian Blyth), 'An Interview with Hélène Cixous', *Paragraph*, 23:3 (November, 'Hélène Cixous'), 338–43

Books and selected articles on Hélène Cixous

Alexandrescu, Liliana, 'Bringing a Historical Character on Stage: *L'Indiade*', trans. by Cornelia Gonla, in *Hélène Cixous: Critical Impressions*, ed. by Lee A. Jacobus and Regina Barreca (Amsterdam: Gordon and Breach, 1999)

Aneja, Ann, 'The Mystic Aspect of L'Ecriture Féminine: Hélène Cixous' *Vivre l'orange*', *Qui Parle* (University of California, Berkeley), 3:1 (Spring 1989), 189–201

—— 'Translating Backwards: Hélène Cixous' *L'Indiade*', *Studies in the Humanities*, 22:12 (December 1995), 50–64

—— 'The Medusa's Slip: Hélène Cixous and the Underpinnings of Ecriture Féminine', *Lit: Literature Interpretation Theory*, 4:1 (1992, 'Hélène Cixous'), 17–28 [repr. in *Hélène Cixous: Critical Impressions*, ed. by Lee A. Jacobus and Regina Barreca (Amsterdam: Gordon and Breach, 1999)]

Banting, Pamela, 'The Body as Pictogram: Rethinking Hélène Cixous' *écriture féminine*', *Textual Practice*, 6:2 (Summer 1992), 225–46

Benmussa, Simone, 'Introduction': "Portrait of Dora": Stage Work and Dream Work', in *Benmussa Directs: Portrait of Dora by Hélène Cixous* (London: Calder/Dallas: Riverrun, 1979)

Binhammer, Katherine, 'Metaphor or Metonymy? The Question of Essentialism in Cixous', *Tessera*, 10 (Summer 1991), 65–79

Birkett, Jennifer, 'The Limits of Language: The Theatre of Hélène Cixous', in *Voices in the Air: French Dramatists and the Resources of Language*, ed. by John Dunkley and Bill Kirton (Glasgow: University of Glasgow French and German Publications, 1992)

Boyman, Anne, 'Dora or the Case of L'Ecriture Féminine', *Qui Parle* (University of California, Berkeley), 3:1 (Spring 1989), 180–8

Brown, Erella, 'The Lake of Seduction: Body, Acting, and Voice in Hélène Cixous's *Portrait de Dora*', *Modern Drama*, 39:4 (Winter 1996), 626–49

Brugmann, Margaret, 'Between the Lines: On the Essayistic Experiments of Hélène Cixous in "Laugh of the Medusa" ', in *The Politics of the Essay: Feminist Perspectives*, ed. by R. Joeres and E. Mittman (Bloomington: Indiana University Press, 1993)

Bryden, Mary, 'Hélène Cixous and Maria Chevska', in *Women and Representation*, ed. by Diana Knight and Judith Still (WIF Publications, 1995)

—— 'Hélène Cixous and the Painterly Eye', in *Thirty Voices in the Feminine*, ed. by Michael Bishop (Amsterdam: Rodopi, 1996)

Calle-Gruber, Mireille, ed., *Du Féminin* (Sainte-Foy: Le Griffon d'Argile/Grenoble: Presses Universitaires de Grenoble, 1992)

—— 'Hélène Cixous: A jamais la musique ou Petit traite d'art poétique pour récit à chanter', in *(en)jeux de la communication romanesque*, ed. by Susan van Dijk and Christa Stevens (Amsterdam: Rodopi, 1994)

—— 'Afterword: Hélène Cixous' Book of Hours, Book of Fortune', trans. by Agnes Conacher and Catherine McGann, in Susan Sellers, ed., *The Hélène Cixous Reader* (London and New York: Routledge, 1994)

—— 'Portrait of the Writing', in *Hélène Cixous Rootprints: Memory and Life Writing*, trans. by Eric Prenowitz (London: Routledge, 1997)

—— 'Chronicle', in *Hélène Cixous Rootprints: Memory and Life Writing*, trans. by Eric Prenowitz (London: Routledge, 1997)

—— 'La Vision prise de vitesse par l'écriture: A propos de *La fiancée juive* d'Hélène Cixous', *Littérature*, 103 (October 1996), 79–93

—— 'Hélène Cixous: Music Forever or Short Treatise on a Poetics for a Story To Be Sung', in *Hélène Cixous: Critical Impressions*, ed. by Lee A. Jacobus and Regina Barreca (Amsterdam: Gordon and Breach, 1999)

—— ed., *Hélène Cixous, croisées d'une oeuvre* (Paris: Galilée, 2000)

—— 'Avant-Propos', in *Hélène Cixous, croisées d'une oeuvre*, ed. by Mireille Calle-Gruber (Paris: Galilée, 2000)

—— 'ou Ce qui ne renonce jamais', in *Hélène Cixous, croisées d'une oeuvre*, ed. by Mireille Calle-Gruber (Paris: Galilée, 2000)

Cameron, Beatrice, 'Letter to Hélène Cixous', *SubStance*, 17 (1977), 159–65

Canning, Charlotte, 'The Critic as Playwright: Performing Hélène Cixous' *Le Nom d'Oedipe*', *Lit: Literature Interpretation Theory*, 4:1 (1992, 'Hélène Cixous'), 43–55 [repr. in *Hélène Cixous: Critical Impressions*, ed. by Lee A. Jacobus and Regina Barreca (Amsterdam: Gordon and Breach, 1999)]

Carpenter, Deborah, 'Hélène Cixous and North African Origin: Writing "L'Orange" ', *Celfan Review*, 6:1 (November 1986), 1–4

—— [Translator's Introduction to 'Her Presence Through Writing'], *Literary Review*, 30:3 (Spring 1987), 441–5

Conley, Verena Andermatt, 'Missexual Mystery', *Diacritics*, 7:2 (Summer 1977), 70–82

—— 'Writing the Letter: The Lower-Case of Hélène Cixous', *Visible Language*, 12:3 (Summer 1978), 305–18

—— 'Hélène Cixous and the Uncovery of a Feminine Language', *Women and Literature*, 7:1 (Winter 1979), 38–48

—— *Hélène Cixous: Writing the Feminine* (Lincoln, NE: University of Nebraska Press, 1984)

—— 'Approaches', *Boundary*, 12:2 (Winter 1984), 1–7

—— 'Saying "Yes" to the Other', *Dalhousie French Studies*, 13 (Autumn–Winter), 92–9

—— 'Hélène Cixous', in *French Novelists Since 1960*, ed. by Catherine Savage Brosman (Detroit: Gale Research, 1989)

—— 'Déliverance', in *Hélène Cixous, chemins d'une écriture*, ed. by Françoise van Rossum-Guyon and Myriam Díaz-Diocaretz (Saint-Denis: Presses Universitaires de Vincennes/Amsterdam: Rodopi, 1990)

—— 'Introduction', in *Reading with Clarice Lispector*, ed. and trans. by Verena Andermatt Conley (Minneapolis: University of Minnesota Press, 1990)

—— 'Hélène Cixous', in *French Women Writers: A Bio-Bibliographical Source Book*, ed. by Eva Martin Sartori and Dorothy Wynne Zimmerman (New York: Greenwood, 1991)

—— 'Introduction', in *Readings: The Poetics of Blanchot, Joyce, Kafka, Kleist, Lispector, and Tsvetayeva*, ed. and trans. by Verena Andermatt Conley (Minneapolis: University of Minnesota Press, 1991)

—— *Hélène Cixous* (Toronto: University of Toronto Press/Hemel Hempstead: Harvester Wheatsheaf, 1992)

—— 'Le Goût du nu', *Lendemains* (Berlin), 13:5, 92–8

—— 'Souffle de vie: hommage à Hélène Cixous', in *Hélène Cixous, croisées d'une oeuvre*, ed. by Mireille Calle-Gruber (Paris: Galilée, 2000)

Cooper, Sarah, 'Genre and Sexuality: Cixous's and Derrida's Textual Performances', in *Powerful Bodies: Performance in French Cultural Studies*, ed. by Victoria Best and Peter Collier (1999)

—— 'The Ethics of Rewriting the Loss of Exile in *Manne aux Mandelstams aux Mandelas*', *Paragraph*, 23:3 (November 2000, 'Hélène Cixous'), 311–23

—— *Relating to Queer Theory: Rereading Sexual Self-Definition with Irigaray, Kristeva, Wittig and Cixous* (Bern: Peter Lang, 2000)

Cornell, Sarah, 'Hélène Cixous' *Le Livre de Promethea*: Paradise Refound', in *Writing Differences: Readings from the Seminar of Hélène Cixous*, ed. by Susan Sellers (Milton Keynes: Open University Press/New York: St Martin's Press, 1988)

—— 'Hélène Cixous and "les Etudes Féminines"', in *The Body and the Text: Hélène Cixous, Reading and Teaching*, ed. by Helen Wilcox, Keith McWatters, Ann Thompson and Linda R. Williams (Hemel Hempstead: Harvester Wheatsheaf, 1990)

Corredor, Eva, 'The Fantastic and the Problem of Re-Presentation in Hélène Cixous' Feminist Fiction', *Papers in Romance*, 4:3 (Autumn 1982), 173–9

Davis, Robert Con, 'Woman as Oppositional Reader: Cixous on Discourse', *Papers on Language and Literature*, 24:3 (Summer 1988), 265–82

—— 'Cixous, Spivak, and Oppositional Theory', *Lit: Literature Interpretation Theory*, 4:1 (1992, 'Hélène Cixous'), 29–42 [repr. in *Hélène Cixous: Critical Impressions*, ed. by Lee A. Jacobus and Regina Barreca (Amsterdam: Gordon and Breach, 1999)]

Defromont, Françoise, 'Metaphorical Thinking and Poetic Writing in Virginia Woolf and Hélène Cixous', in *The Body and the Text: Hélène*

Cixous, Reading and Teaching, ed. by Helen Wilcox, Keith McWatters, Ann Thompson and Linda R. Williams (Hemel Hempstead: Harvester Wheatsheaf, 1990)

Deleuze, Gilles, 'L'Ecriture stroboscopique', *Le Monde* (11 August 1972)

Derrida, Jacques, 'Fourmis', in *Lectures de la Différence Sexuelle*, ed. by Mara Negron (Paris: Des femmes, 1994)

—— 'Foreword', trans. by Eric Prenowitz, in Susan Sellers, ed., *The Hélène Cixous Reader* (London and New York: Routledge, 1994) [Translated excerpt from 'Fourmis' (1994)]

—— 'Fourmis', in *Hélène Cixous Rootprints: Memory and Life Writing*, trans. by Eric Prenowitz (London: Routledge, 1997) [Translated excerpt from 'Fourmis' (1994)]

—— 'H. C. Pour la vie, c'est à dire', in *Hélène Cixous, croisées d'une oeuvre*, ed. by Mireille Calle-Gruber (Paris: Galilée, 2000)

Dobson, Julia, 'The Scene of Writing: The Representation of Poetic Identity in Cixous' Recent Theatre', *Theatre Research International*, 23:3 (Autumn 1998), 255–60

—— 'Asserting Identities: The Theatres of Marina Tsvetaeva and Hélène Cixous', *Forum for Modern Language Studies*, 35:3 (July 1999), 261–9

—— 'At the Time of Writing Theatre: Hélène Cixous's Absolute Present', *Paragraph*, 23:3 (November 2000, 'Hélène Cixous'), 270–81

—— 'Hélène Cixous, *Tambours sur la digue*, performed by the Théâtre du Soleil, Paris, May 2000: A First Response', *Paragraph*, 23:3 (November 2000, 'Hélène Cixous'), 344–9

—— *Hélène Cixous and the Theatre: The Scene of Writing* (Bern: Peter Lang, 2002)

Etienne, Marie-France, 'Disembodied World, Song of Exile: *Le Nom d'Oedipe: chant du corps inderdit*', *Dalhousie French Studies*, 28 (1994), 131–40

Evans, Martha Noel, '*Portrait of Dora*: Freud's Case History as Reviewed by Hélène Cixous', *SubStance*, 36 (1982), 64–71

Fisher, Claudine Guégam, 'Hélène Cixous' Window of Daring through Clarice Lispector's Voice', in *Continental Latin-American and Francophone Women Writers*, ed. by Eunice Myers and Ginette Adamson (Lanham: University Presses of America, 1987)

—— *La Cosmogonie d'Hélène Cixous* (Amsterdam: Rodopi, 1988)

—— 'Cixous' North/South Feminist Dichotomy', *Lit: Literature Interpretation Theory*, 2:3 (1991), 231–7

—— 'Cixous' Concept of "Brushing" as a Gift', in *Hélène Cixous: Critical Impressions*, ed. by Lee A. Jacobus and Regina Barreca (Amsterdam: Gordon and Breach, 1999)

Fitz, Earl E., 'Hélène Cixous's Debt to Clarice Lispector: The Case of *Vivre l'orange* and "l'écriture féminine" ', *Revue de Littérature comparée*, 64:1 (January–March 1990), 235–49

Franks, Helen, 'Dying to Write: Space and Death in the Poetics of Hélène Cixous', in *Cemeteries and Spaces of Death*, ed. by Darnetta Bell and Kevin Bongiorni (Riverside, CA: Xenos, 1996)

Frappier-Mazur, Lucienne, 'Metaphor and Discourse, Marginality and Mastery: Clément and Cixous's Reading of Freud's Dora', in *Thematics Reconsidered*, ed. by Frank Trommler (Amsterdam: Rodopi, 1995)

Freedman, Barbara, 'Plus-Corps-Donc-Plus-Ecriture: Hélène Cixous and the Mind-Body Problem', *Paragraph*, 11:1 (March 1988), 58–70

Freeman, Sandra, 'Bisexuality in Cixous's *Le Nom d'Oedipe*', *Theatre Research International*, 23:3 (Autumn 1998), 242–8

Gilbert, Sandra, 'Introduction: A Tarantella of Theory', in Hélène Cixous and Catherine Clément, *The Newly Born Woman*, trans. by Betsy Wing (Minneapolis: University of Minnesota Press, 1986)

Gough, Val, 'The Lesbian Christ: Body Politics in Hélène Cixous's *Le Livre de Promethea*', in *Body Matters: Feminism, Textuality, Corporeality*, ed. by Avril Horner and Angela Keane (Manchester: Manchester University Press, 2000)

Graver, David, 'The Théâtre du Soleil, Part Three: The Production of *Sihanouk*', *New Theatre Quarterly*, 2:7 (August 1986), 212–15

Hammer, Stephanie, 'In the Name of the Rose: Gertrud Kolmar, Hélène Cixous and the Poerotics of Jewish Femininity', in *Transforming the Centre, Eroding the Margins: Essays on Ethnic and Cultural Boundaries in German-Speaking Countries*, ed. by Dagmar C. G. Lorenz and Renate S. Posthofen (Columbia, SC: Camden House, 1998)

Hanrahan, Mairéad, 'Hélène Cixous' *Dedans*: The Father Makes an Exit', in *Contemporary French Fiction by Women: Feminist Perspectives*, ed. by Margaret Atack and Phil Powrie (Manchester: Manchester University Press, 1990)

—— 'Une Porte du *Portrait du soleil* ou la succulence du sujet', in *Hélène Cixous, chemins d'une écriture*, ed. by Françoise van Rossum-Guyon and Myriam Díaz-Diocaretz (Saint-Denis: Presses Universitaires de Vincennes/Amsterdam: Rodopi, 1990)

—— 'Cixous's *Portrait of Dora*, or Cooking the Books of Psychoanalysis', *Women in French Studies*, 5 (Winter 1997), 271–9

—— 'Cixous's *Portrait de Dora*: The Play of Whose Voice?', *Modern Language Review*, 93 (1998), 48–58

—— 'Genet and Cixous: The InterSext', *French Review*, 72:4 (March 1999), 719–29

—— 'Le texte de l'autre texte, ou le livre délivre', in *Hélène Cixous, croisées d'une oeuvre*, ed. by Mireille Calle-Gruber (Paris: Galilée, 2000)

—— 'Oublire: Cixous's Poetics of Forgetting', *Symposium*, 54:2 (Summer 2000), 77–89

—— 'Of Altobiography', *Paragraph*, 23:3 (November 2000, 'Hélène Cixous'), 282–95

—— 'Cixous's *Le Livre de Promethea*: A Diary in an Other Form', *French Studies*, 55:2 (April 2001), 195–206

Johnson, Erica, 'Incomplete Histories and Hélène Cixous's *L'Histoire terrible mais inachevée de Norodom Sihanouk, roi du Cambodge*', *Texas Studies in Literature and Language*, 42:2 (Summer 2000), 118–34

Jones, Ann, 'Writing the Body: Toward an Understanding of "L'Ecriture Féminine" ', *Feminist Studies*, 7:2 (Summer 1981), 247–63 [repr. in *Making a Difference: Feminist Literary Criticism*, ed. by Gayle Greene and Coppelia Kahn (London: Methuen, 1985); repr. in *The New Feminist Criticism: Essays on Women, Literature and Theory*, ed. by Elaine Showalter (New York: Pantheon, 1985); repr. in *Feminist Literary Theory*, ed. by Mary Eagleton (Oxford: Blackwell, 1986)]

Jouve, Nicole Ward, 'Oranges et sources: Colette et Hélène Cixous', in *Hélène Cixous, chemins d'une écriture*, ed. by Françoise van Rossum-Guyon and Myriam Díaz-Diocaretz (Saint-Denis: Presses Universitaires de Vincennes/Amsterdam: Rodopi, 1990)

—— 'Hélène Cixous: From Inner Theatre to World Theatre', in *The Body and the Text: Hélène Cixous, Reading and Teaching*, ed. by Helen Wilcox, Keith McWatters, Ann Thompson and Linda R. Williams (Hemel Hempstead: Harvester Wheatsheaf, 1990) [repr. in Nicole Ward Jouve, *White Woman Speaks with Forked Tongue: Criticism as Autobiography* (London: Routledge, 1991)]

—— 'The Faces of Power: Hélène Cixous', *Our Voices Ourselves: Women Writing for the French Theatre* (New York: Peter Lang, 1991)

—— 'Hélène Cixous Across the Atlantic: The Medusa as Projection?', in *Traveling Theory: France and the United States*, ed. by Ieme van der Poel and Sophie Bertho (Madison, NJ: Fairleigh Dickinson University, 1999)

—— 'Le plus veil enfant: figures du destin dans le théâtre d'Hélène Cixous', in *Hélène Cixous, croisées d'une oeuvre*, ed. by Mireille Calle-Gruber (Paris: Galilée, 2000)

Juncker, C., 'Writing (with) Cixous', *College English*, 50:4 (1988), 424–36

Kamuf, Peggy, 'To Give Place: Semi-Approaches to Hélène Cixous', *Yale French Studies*, 87 (1995), 68–89 [repr. in *Another Look, Another*

Woman: Retranslations of French Feminism, ed. by Lynne Huffer (New Haven, CT: Yale University Press, 1995)]

—— 'Souris', in *Hélène Cixous, croisées d'une oeuvre*, ed. by Mireille Calle-Gruber (Paris: Galilée, 2000)

Klobucka, Anna, 'Hélène Cixous and the *Hour of Clarice Lispector*', *Sub-Stance*, 23:1 [73] (1994), 41–62

Kogan, Vivian, 'I Want Vulva! Hélène Cixous and the Poetics of the Body', *L'Esprit créature*, 25:2 (Summer 1985), 73–85

Lamar, Celita, 'Norodom Sihanouk, A Hero of Our Times: Character Development in Hélène Cixous' Cambodian Epic', in *From the Bard to Broadway*, ed. by Karelisa Hartigan (Lanham: University Presses of America, 1987)

Lamont, Rosette C., '*The Terrible But Unended Story of Norodom Sihanouk: King of Cambodia* by Hélène Cixous', *Performing Arts Journal*, 10:1 (1986), 46–50

—— 'The Reverse Side of a Portrait: The Dora of Freud and Cixous', in *Feminine Focus: The New Women Playwrights*, ed. by Enoch Brater (Oxford: Oxford University Press, 1989)

—— 'Ariane Mnouchkine/Hélène Cixous: The Meeting of Two Chimeras', in *Hélène Cixous: Critical Impressions*, ed. by Lee A. Jacobus and Regina Barreca (Amsterdam: Gordon and Breach, 1999)

Lie, Sissel, 'Pour une lécture féminine', in *The Body and the Text: Hélène Cixous, Reading and Teaching*, ed. by Helen Wilcox, Keith McWatters, Ann Thompson and Linda R. Williams (Hemel Hempstead: Harvester Wheatsheaf, 1990)

—— 'Life Makes Text from My Body: A Reading of Hélène Cixous' *La Venue à l'écriture*', in *Hélène Cixous: Critical Impressions*, ed. by Lee A. Jacobus and Regina Barreca (Amsterdam: Gordon and Breach, 1999)

—— 'L'image de l'artiste – Hélène Cixous', in *Hélène Cixous, croisées d'une oeuvre*, ed. by Mireille Calle-Gruber (Paris: Galilée, 2000)

Lindsay, Cecile, 'Body/Language: French Feminist Utopias', *The French Review*, 60:1 (October 1986), 46–55

Lydon, Mary, 'Re-Translating no Re-Reading no, Rather: Rejoycing (with) Hélène Cixous', in *Another Look, Another Woman: Retranslations of French Feminism*, ed. by Lynne Huffer (1995)

—— 'Affinités électives: l'art poétique d'Hélène Cixous', in *Hélène Cixous, croisées d'une oeuvre*, ed. by Mireille Calle-Gruber (Paris: Galilée, 2000)

MacCannall, Juliet Flower, Judith Pike and Lollie Groth, 'Introduction', in *The Terrible but Unfinished Story of Norodom Sihanouk, King of*

Cambodia, trans. by Juliet Flower MacCannell, Judith Pike and Lollie Groth (Lincoln, NE: University of Nebraska Press, 1998)

MacGillivray, Catherine A.F., 'Introduction: "The Political Is – (and the) Poetical" ', in *Manna for the Mandelstams for the Mandelas*, trans. by Catherine A. F. MacGillivray (Minneapolis: University of Minnesota Press, 1994)

—— 'Translator's Preface', *Voile Noire Voile Blanche/Black Sail White Sail*, *New Literary History*, 25:2 (Spring 1994), 219–21

—— 'Translator's Preface: Translating Hélène Cixous's Book of Days', in *FirstDays of the Year*, trans. by Catherine A. F. MacGillivray (Minneapolis: University of Minnesota Press, 1998)

Manners, Marilyn, 'The Doxies of Daughterhood: Plath, Cixous, and the Father', *Comparative Literature*, 48:2 (Spring 1996), 150–71

—— 'The Vagaries of Flight in Hélène Cixous's *Le Troisième Corps*', *French Forum*, 23:1 (January 1998), 101–14

—— 'Hélène Cixous Names Woman, Mother, Other: "a feminine plural like me" ', in *Hélène Cixous: Critical Impressions*, ed. by Lee A. Jacobus and Regina Barreca (Amsterdam: Gordon and Breach, 1999)

Marks, Elaine, 'Woman and Literature in France', *Signs*, 3:4 (Summer 1978), 832–42

Miller, Judith, 'Jean Cocteau and Hélène Cixous: Oedipus', in *Drama, Sex and Politics*, ed. by James Redmond (Cambridge: Cambridge University Press, 1985)

Moi, Toril, 'Hélène Cixous: An Imaginary Utopia', in *Sexual/Textual Politics: Feminist Literary Theory* (London: Methuen, 1985)

Moss, Jane, 'Women's Theater in France', *Signs*, 12:3 (Spring 1987), 554–9

Motard-Noar, Martine, *Les Fictions d'Hélène Cixous: Une autre langue de femme* (Lexington: French Forum, 1991)

—— 'From Persephone to Demeter: A Feminist Experience in Cixous's Fiction', in *Images of Persephone: Feminist Readings in Western Literature*, ed. by Elizabeth T. Hayes (Gainesville, FL: University Press of Florida, 1994)

—— 'Manne ou Man: Où en est l'écriture d'Hélène Cixous?', *The French Review*, 66:2 (December 1992), 286–94

—— 'Hélène Cixous', in *The Contemporary Novel in France*, ed. by William Thompson (1995)

—— 'Reading and Writing the Other: Criticism as Felicity', *Lit: Literature Interpretation Theory*, 4:1 (1992, 'Hélène Cixous'), 57–68 [repr. in

Hélène Cixous: Critical Impressions, ed. by Lee A. Jacobus and Regina Barreca (Amsterdam: Gordon and Breach, 1999)]

Noonan, Mary, 'Performing the Voice of Writing in the In-Between, Hélène Cixous's *La Ville parjure*', *Nottingham French Studies*, 38 (1999), 67–79

Obussier, Claire, 'Synaesthesia in Cixous and Barthes', in *Women and Representation*, ed. by Diana Knight and Judith Still (1995)

Pavlides, Merope, 'Restructuring the Traditional: An Examination of Hélène Cixous' *Le Nom d'Oedipe*', in *Within the Dramatic Spectrum*, ed. by Karelisa Hartigan (Lanham: University Presses of America, 1986)

Penrod, Lynn Kettler, 'Translating Hélène Cixous: French Feminism(s) and Anglo-American Feminist Theory', *TTR: Traduction, Terminologie, Rédaction* (Montreal), 6:2 (1993), 39–54

—— *Hélène Cixous* (New York: Twayne, 1996)

Picard, Anne-Marie, '*L'Indiade*: Ariane and Hélène Conjugate Dreams', *Modern Drama*, 32:1 (March 1989), 24–38

—— '*L'Indiade ou l'Inde de leurs rêves*', *Dalhousie French Studies*, 17 (Autumn–Winter 1989), 17–26

—— '*Le Père de l'Écriture*: Writing Within the Secret Father', in *Hélène Cixous: Critical Impressions*, ed. by Lee A. Jacobus and Regina Barreca (Amsterdam: Gordon and Breach, 1999)

—— 'Cette tombe est une source, le père de l'écriture', in *Hélène Cixous, croisées d'une oeuvre*, ed. by Mireille Calle-Gruber (Paris: Galilée, 2000)

Plate, Liedeke, ' "I Come from a Woman": Writing, Gender, and Authorship in Hélène Cixous's *The Book of Promethea*', *Journal of Narrative Technique*, 26:2 (Spring 1996), 158–71

Plate, S. Brent, and Edna M. Rodriguez Mangual, 'The Gift That Stops Giving: Hélène Cixous's "Gift" and the Shunammite Woman', *Biblical Interpretation*, 7:2 (April 1999), 113–32

Prenowitz, Eric, 'Aftermaths', in *Hélène Cixous Rootprints: Memory and Life Writing*, trans. by Eric Prenowitz (London: Routledge, 1997)

—— 'Approches d'un départ (reste)', in *Hélène Cixous, croisées d'une oeuvre*, ed. by Mireille Calle-Gruber (Paris: Galilée, 2000)

Rabine, Leslie, 'Ecriture Féminine as Metaphor', *Cultural Critique*, 8 (Winter 1987–88), 19–44

Rossum-Guyon, Françoise van, and Myriam Díaz-Diocaretz, eds, *Hélène Cixous, chemins d'une écriture* (Saint-Denis: Presses Universitaires de Vincennes/Amsterdam: Rodopi, 1990)

—— and Myriam Díaz-Diocaretz, 'Présentation: l'oeuvre d'Hélène Cixous', in *Hélène Cixous, chemins d'une écriture*, ed. by Françoise van

Rossum-Guyon and Myriam Díaz-Diocaretz (Saint-Denis: Presses Universitaires de Vincennes/Amsterdam: Rodopi, 1990)

—— *Le Cœur critique: Butor, Simon, Kristeva, Cixous* (Amsterdam: Rodopi, 1997)

Running-Johnson, Cynthia, 'The Medusa's Tale: Feminine Writing and "La Genet"', *Romantic Review*, 80:3 (May 1989), 438–95

—— 'Themes in Drama II: Feminine Writing and Its Theatrical "Other"', in *Women in Theatre*, ed. by James Redmond (Cambridge: Cambridge University Press, 1989)

—— '*La Ville parjure ou le réveil des Erinyes*: Cixous' Theatrical Reawakening', in *Thirty Voices in the Feminine*, ed. by Michael Bishop (Amsterdam: Rodopi, 1996)

—— 'The Self and "Other(s)" in Cixous' *Sihanouk*', in *Hélène Cixous: Critical Impressions*, ed. by Lee A. Jacobus and Regina Barreca (Amsterdam: Gordon and Breach, 1999)

Rye, Gill, 'Reading Identities with Kristeva and Cixous in Christiane Baroche's *L'Hiver de beauté*', *Paragraph*, 19:2 (July 1996), 98–113

—— 'Weaving the Reader into Text: The Authority and Generosity of Modern Women Writers', *Women in French Studies*, 5 (Winter 1997), 161–72

—— 'Time for Change: Re(con)figuring Maternity in Contemporary French Literature (Baroche, Cixous, Constant, Redonnet)', *Paragraph*, 21:3 (November 1998), 354–75

—— 'Agony or Ecstasy? Reading Cixous's Recent Fiction', *Paragraph*, 23:3 (November 2000, 'Hélène Cixous'), 296–310

—— *Reading for Change: Interactions Between Text and Identity in Contemporary French Women's Writing (Baroche, Cixous, Constant)* (Bern: Peter Lang, 2001)

Salesne, Pierre, 'Hélène Cixous' *Ou l'art de l'innocence*: The Path to You', in *Writing Differences: Readings from the Seminar of Hélène Cixous*, ed. by Susan Sellers (Milton Keynes: Open University Press/New York: St Martin's Press, 1988)

—— 'L'émoi d'Hélène Cixous en langues d'autres', in *Hélène Cixous, chemins d'une écriture*, ed. by Françoise van Rossum-Guyon and Myriam Díaz-Diocaretz (Saint-Denis: Presses Universitaires de Vincennes/Amsterdam: Rodopi, 1990)

Sandré, Marguerite, and Christa Stevens, 'Bibliographie des oeuvres d'Hélène Cixous', in *Hélène Cixous, chemins d'une écriture*, ed. by Françoise van Rossum-Guyon and Myriam Díaz-Diocaretz (Saint-Denis: Presses Universitaires de Vincennes/Amsterdam: Rodopi, 1990)

—— and Eric Prenowitz, 'Hélène Cixous, Bibliography', in *Hélène Cixous Rootprints: Memory and Life Writing*, trans. by Eric Prenowitz (London: Routledge, 1997)

Sankovitch, Tilde, 'Hélène Cixous: The Pervasive Myth', in *French Women Writers and the Book: Myths of Access and Desire* (Syracuse: Syracuse University Press, 1988)

Santellani, Violette, 'Men More Than Men', in *Hélène Cixous: Critical Impressions*, ed. by Lee A. Jacobus and Regina Barreca (Amsterdam: Gordon and Breach, 1999)

Savona, Jeanette Laillou, 'French Feminism and Theatre: An Introduction', *Modern Drama*, 27:4 (December 1984), 540–5

—— 'In Search of Feminist Theater: Portrait of Dora', in *Feminine Focus: The New Women Playwrights*, ed. by Enoch Brater (Oxford: Oxford University Press, 1989)

—— '*Portrait de Dora* d'Hélène Cixous: A la recherche d'un théâtre féministe', in *Hélène Cixous, chemins d'une écriture*, ed. by Françoise van Rossum-Guyon and Myriam Díaz-Diocaretz (Saint-Denis: Presses Universitaires de Vincennes/Amsterdam: Rodopi, 1990)

—— 'La Multisexualité de l'amour: de *Tancrède continue* au *Livre de Promethea*', in *Hélène Cixous, croisées d'une oeuvre*, ed. by Mireille Calle-Gruber (Paris: Galilée, 2000)

Scheie, Timothy, Body Trouble: Corporeal "Presence" and Performative Identity in Cixous's and Mnouchkine's *L'Indiade ou L'Inde de leur rêves*', *Theatre Journal*, 46 (1994), 31–44

Schrift, Alan D., 'On the Gynecology of Morals: Nietzsche and Cixous on the Logic of the Gift', in *Nietzsche and the Feminine*, ed. by Peter J. Burgard (Charlottesville, VA: University Press of Virginia, 1995)

—— 'Logics of the Gift in Cixous and Nietzsche: Can We Still Be Generous?', *Angelaki* (Oxford), 6:2 (August 2001), 113–23

Scott, H. Jill, 'Loving the Other: Subjectivities of Proximity in Cixous's *Book of Promethea*', *World Literature Today*, 69 (1995), 29–34

Sellers, Susan, 'Writing Woman: Hélène Cixous' Political "Sexts"', *Women's Studies International Forum*, 9:4 (1986), 443–7

—— ed., *Writing Differences: Readings from the Seminar of Hélène Cixous* (Milton Keynes: Open University Press/New York: St Martin's Press, 1988)

—— 'Biting the Teacher's Apple: Opening Doors for Women in Higher Education', in *Teaching Women: Feminism and English Studies*, ed. by Ann Thompson and Helen Wilcox (Manchester: Manchester University Press, 1989)

——— 'Learning to Read the Feminine', in *The Body and the Text: Hélène Cixous, Reading and Teaching*, ed. by Helen Wilcox, Keith McWatters, Ann Thompson and Linda R. Williams (Hemel Hempstead: Harvester Wheatsheaf, 1990)

——— 'Blowing up the Law', 'Masculine and Feminine', 'The Mother's Voice', 'Woman's Abasement', 'Writing the Other', 'Writing Other Worlds', in *Language and Sexual Difference: Feminist Writing in France* (Basingstoke: Macmillan/New York: St Martin's Press, 1991)

——— ed., *The Hélène Cixous Reader* (London and New York: Routledge, 1994)

——— *Hélène Cixous: Authorship, Autobiography and Love* (Cambridge: Polity Press, 1996)

——— 'Virginia Woolf's Diaries and Letters', in *The Cambridge Companion to Virginia Woolf*, ed. by Sue Roe and Susan Sellers (Cambridge: Cambridge University Press, 2000)

Shiach, Morag, 'Their "Symbolic" Exists, it Holds Power – We, the Sowers of Disorder, Know it Only Too Well', in *Feminism and Psychoanalysis*, ed. by Teresa Brennan (London: Routledge, 1989)

——— *Hélène Cixous: A Politics of Writing* (London: Routledge, 1991)

——— 'La peur et l'espoir dans l'écriture féministe contemporaine', in *Hélène Cixous, croisées d'une oeuvre*, ed. by Mireille Calle-Gruber (Paris: Galilée, 2000)

——— 'Millennial Fears: Fear, Hope and Transformation in Contemporary Feminist Writing', *Paragraph*, 23:3 (November 2000, 'Hélène Cixous'), 324–37

Silverstein, Marc, 'Body-Presence: Cixous' Phenomenology of Theater', *Theatre Journal*, 43:4 (December 1991), 507–16

Singer, Linda, 'True Confessions: Cixous and Foucault on Sexuality and Power', in *The Thinking Muse: Feminism and Modern French Philosophy*, ed. by Jeffner Allen and Marion Young (Bloomington: Indiana University Press, 1989)

Singleton, Brian, 'Body Politic(s): The Actor as Mask in the Théâtre du Soleil's *Les Atrides* and *La Ville Parjure*', *Modern Drama*, 39:4 (Winter 1996), 618–25

Spivak, Gayatri Chakravorty, 'French Feminism in an International Frame', *Yale French Studies*, 62 (1981), 154–84; repr. in *In Other Worlds: Essays in Cultural Politics* (New York: Methuen, 1987)

Stanton, Domna C., 'Language and Revolution: The Franco-American Dis-Connection', in *The Future of Difference*, ed. by Hester Eisenstein and Alice Jardine (Boston, MA: Hall, 1980)

——— 'Difference on Trial: A Critique of the Maternal Metaphor in Cixous, Irigaray and Kristeva', in *The Poetics of Gender*, ed. by Nancy K. Miller (New York: Columbia University Press, 1986)

Stevens, Christa, 'Hélène Cixous and the Need of Portraying: on *Portrait du Soleil*', in *Hélène Cixous: Critical Impressions*, ed. by Lee A. Jacobus and Regina Barreca (Amsterdam: Gordon and Breach, 1999)

——— *L'Ecriture solaire d'Hélène Cixous: Travail du texte et histoires du sujet dans* Portrait du soleil (Amsterdam: Rodopi, 1999)

Still, Judith, 'A Feminine Economy: Some Preliminary Thoughts', in *The Body and the Text: Hélène Cixous, Reading and Teaching*, ed. by Helen Wilcox, Keith McWatters, Ann Thompson and Linda R. Williams (Hemel Hempstead: Harvester Wheatsheaf, 1990)

——— 'The Gift: Hélène Cixous and Jacques Derrida', in *Hélène Cixous: Critical Impressions*, ed. by Lee A. Jacobus and Regina Barreca (Amsterdam: Gordon and Breach, 1999)

Suleiman, Susan Rubin, '(Re)Writing the Body: The Politics and Poetics of Female Eroticism', in *The Female Body in Western Culture: Contemporary Perspectives* (Cambridge, MA: Harvard University Press, 1991)

——— 'Writing Past the Wall or the Passion According to H. C.', in Hélène Cixous, *Coming to Writing and Other Essays* (Cambridge, MA: Harvard University Press, 1991)

Thomas, Sue, 'Difference, Intersubjectivity and Agency in the Colonial and Decolonizing Spaces of Cixous's "Sorties"', *Hypatia*, 9 (1994), 53–69

Turner, Pamela, 'Hélène Cixous: A Space Between – Women and (Their) Language', *Lit: Literature Interpretation Theory*, 4:1 (1992, 'Hélène Cixous'), 69–77 [repr. in *Hélène Cixous: Critical Impressions*, ed. by Lee A. Jacobus and Regina Barreca (Amsterdam: Gordon and Breach, 1999)]

Walsh, Lisa, 'Writing (into) the Symbolic: The Maternal Metaphor in Hélène Cixous', in *Language and Liberation: Feminism, Philosophy, and Language*, ed. by Christina Hendricks and Oliver Kelly (Albany, NY: State University of New York Press, 1999)

Wilcox, Helen, Keith McWatters, Ann Thompson and Linda R. Williams, eds, *The Body and the Text: Hélène Cixous, Reading and Teaching* (Hemel Hempstead: Harvester Wheatsheaf, 1990)

Willis, Sharon, 'Portrait de Dora: The Unseen and the Un-Scene', *Theatre Journal*, 37:3 (October 1985), 287–301

——— 'Mis-Translation: *Vivre l'orange*', *Studies in the Novel*, 18:4 (Winter 1986), 76–83 [repr. *SubStance*, 16:1 (1987), 76–83]

—— 'Mistranslation, Missed Translation: Hélène Cixous' *Vivre l'orange*', in *Rethinking Translation: Discourse, Subjectivity, Ideology*, ed. by Lawrence Venuti (London: Routledge, 1992)

Wilson, Ann, 'History and Hysteria: Writing the Body in "Portrait of Dora" and "Signs of Life"', *Modern Drama*, 32:1 (March 1989), 73–88

Wilson, Emma, 'Hélène Cixous: An Erotics of the Feminine', in *French Erotic Fiction: Women's Desiring Writing 1880–1990*, ed. by Alex Hughes and Kate Ince (Oxford: Berg, 1996)

—— *Sexuality and the Reading Encounter: Identity and Desire in Proust, Duras, Tournier and Cixous* (Oxford: Clarendon Press, 1996)

—— 'Identification and Melancholia: The Inner Cinema of Hélène Cixous', *Paragraph*, 23:3 (November 2000, 'Hélène Cixous'), 258–69

Wing, Betsy, 'A Translator's Imaginary Choices', in *The Book of Promethea*, trans. by Betsy Wing (Lincoln, NE: University of Nebraska Press, 1991)

Wiseman, Susan, '"Femininity" and the Intellectual in Sontag and Cixous', in *The Body and the Text: Hélène Cixous, Reading and Teaching*, ed. by Helen Wilcox, Keith McWatters, Ann Thompson and Linda R. Williams (Hemel Hempstead: Harvester Wheatsheaf, 1990)

Worsham, Lynn, 'Writing against Writing: The Predicament of Ecriture Féminine in Composition Studies', in *Contending With Words: Composition and Rhetoric in a Postmodern Age*, ed. by Patricia Harkin and John Schilb (New York: Modern Languages Association of America, 1991)

Yee, Jennifer, 'The Colonial Outsider: "Malgerie" in Hélène Cixous' *Les Rêveries de la femme sauvage*', *Tulsa Studies in Women's Literature*, 20:2 (Autumn 2001), 189–200

Index

MORE PHILOSOPHY FROM CONTINUUM

THE GREAT THINKERS A-Z
Edited by Julian Baggini and Jeremy Stangroom

HB • 0 82646754 7 • £45.00/$75.00
PB • 0 8264 6742 3 • £9.99/$15.95 • 256pp • 2004

WHAT PHILOSOPHERS THINK
Edited by Julian Baggini and Jeremy Stangroom

HB • 0 8264 6754 7 • £45.00/$85.00
PB • 0 8264 6180 8 • £9.99/$14.95 • 256pp • 2003

WHAT PHILOSOPHY IS
Edited by Havi Cavel and David Gamez

HB • 0 8264 7241 9 • £45.00/$85.00
PB • 0 8264 7242 7 • £9.99/$15.95 • 352pp • 2004

INFINITE THOUGHT
Truth and the Return of Philosophy
Alain Badiou

HB • 0 8264 6724 5 • £16.99/$19.95
PB • 0 8264 7320 2 • £9.99/$19.95 • 208pp • 2004

TIME FOR REVOLUTION
Antonio Negri

HB • 0 8264 5931 5 • £16.99/$29.95
PB • 0 8264 7328 8 • £9.99/$19.95 • 304pp • 2004

KILLING FREUD
Twentieth Century Culture and the Death of Psychoanalysis
Todd Dufresne

HB • 0 8264 6893 4 • £16.99/$19.95 • 224pp • 2003

LIFE.AFTER.THEORY
Interviews with Jacques Derrida, Frank Kermode, Toril Moi
and Christopher Norris
Edited by Michael Payne and John Schad

HB • 0 8264 6565 X • £16.99/$19.95
PB • 0 8264 7317 2 • £9.99/$12.95 • 208pp • 2004